Rose Porter

Immortelles in Loving Memory of England's Poet Laureate

Selections from the Writings of Alfred, Lord Tennyson

Rose Porter

Immortelles in Loving Memory of England's Poet Laureate
Selections from the Writings of Alfred, Lord Tennyson

ISBN/EAN: 9783337377168

Printed in Europe, USA, Canada, Australia, Japan

Cover: Foto ©Thomas Meinert / pixelio.de

More available books at **www.hansebooks.com**

IMMORTELLES

IN LOVING MEMORY OF ENGLAND'S POET LAUREATE

Selections From The Writings Of Alfred, Lord Tennyson

Selected And Arranged By
ROSE PORTER

BOSTON
D. LOTHROP COMPANY
1893

CONTENTS.

PRELUDE.

THE lights begin to twinkle from the rocks;
The long day wanes; the slow moon climbs. . .
. . . .
. . . Come, my friends,
'Tis not too late to seek a newer world.
Push off, and sitting well in order smite
The sounding furrows; for my purpose holds
To sail beyond the sunset, and the baths
Of all the western stars. . . .
. . . .
It may be we shall touch the Happy Isles.

Part First.

AN OLIO OF TREASURES.

LIFE.

I WILL drink
Life to the lees: all times I have enjoyed
Greatly, have suffered greatly, both with those
That loved me, and alone.

.   .   .   .

I am a part of all that I have met;
Yet all experience is an arch wherethrough
Gleams that untraveled world, whose margin
    fades
Forever and forever when I move.
How dull it is to pause, to make an end,
To rust unburnished, not to shine in use!
As though to breathe were life.   Life piled on
    life
Were all too little, and of one to me
Little remains; but every hour is saved
From that eternal silence, something more —
A bringer of new things.   .   .   .

————

My own dim life shall teach me this:
That life shall live forever more.

1

PRAYER.

More things are wrought by prayer
Than this world dreams of. Wherefore, let
  thy voice
Rise like a fountain for me night and day.
For what are men better than sheep or goats
That nourish a blind life within the brain,
If, knowing God, they lift not hands of prayer
Both for themselves and those who call them
  friend?
For so the whole round earth is every way
Bound by gold chains about the feet of God.

JUDGE NOT.

He that wrongs his friend
Wrongs himself more, and ever bears about
A silent court of justice in his breast,
Himself the judge and jury, and himself
The prisoner at the bar, ever condemn'd:
And that drags down his life, then comes what
  comes
Hereafter.

One shriek of hate would jar all the hymns of
  Heaven.

LAST WORDS.

EVERY man at time of death
Would fain set forth some saying that may
    live
After his death and better humankind;
For death gives life's last words a power to
    live,
And, like the stone-cut epitaph, remain
After the vanished voice, and speak to men.

––––

A DEAD man's dying wish should be of weight.

––––

PATIENCE.

WAIT, and Love himself will bring
The drooping flower of knowledge changed to
    fruit
Of wisdom. Wait: my faith is large in Time,
And that which shapes it to some perfect end.
Will some one say, Then why not ill for good?
Why took ye not your pastime? To that
    man
My work shall answer, since I knew the right
And did it; for a man is not as God,
But then most Godlike being most a man.

CIRCUMSTANCE.

Two children in two neighbor villages
  Playing mad pranks along the healthy leas ;
Two strangers meeting at a festival ;
Two lovers whispering by an orchard wall ;
    Two lives bound fast in one with golden
      ease ;
    Two graves grass-green beside a gray church-
      tower,
Wash'd with still rains and daisy-blossomed ;
Two children in one hamlet born and bred ;
    So runs the round of life from hour to hour.

THE PATH OF DUTY.

Not once or twice in our rough island story,
The path of duty was the way to glory ;
He that walks it, only thirsting
For the right, and learns to deaden
Love of self, before his journey closes,
He shall find the stubborn thistle bursting
Into glossy purples, which out-redden
All voluptuous garden roses.
Not once or twice in our fair island story,
The path of duty was the way to glory.

HE, that ever following her commands,
On with toil of heart and knees and hands,
Thro' the long gorge to the far light has
    won
His path upward, and prevail'd,
Shall find the toppling crags of Duty scaled
Are close upon the shining tablelands
To which our God himself is moon and sun.

———

THESE are the days of advance, the works of the
    men of mind.

———

ONWARD.

NOT of the sunlight,
Not of the moonlight,
Not of the starlight!
O, young Mariner,
Down to the haven,
Call your companions,
Launch your vessel,
And crowd your canvas
And, ere it vanishes
Over the margin,
After it, follow it;
Follow the gleam.

THE WILL.

To sleep I give my powers away ; .
  My will is bondsman to the dark ;
  I sit within a helmless bark,
And with my heart I muse and say :

O heart, how fares it with thee now,
  That thou shouldst fail from thy desire,
  Who scarcely darest to inquire
" What is it makes me beat so low ? "

Something it is which thou hast lost,
  Some pleasure from thine early years,
  Break, thou deep vase of chilling tears,
That grief hath shaken into frost !

Such clouds of nameless trouble cross
  All night below the darken'd eyes ;
  With morning wakes the will, and cries,
"Thou shalt not be the fool of loss."

———

THE highest-mounted mind
Still sees the sacred morning spread
The silent summit overhead.

DEATH AND LOVE.

SULLEN-SEEMING Death may give
More life to Love than is or ever was
In our low world, where yet 'tis sweet to live.

———

A SHADOW flits before me,
  Not thou, but like to thee.
Ah, Christ! that it were possible
  For one short hour to see
The souls we loved, that they might tell us
  What and where they be.

———

FLOWERS.

FLOWER in the crannied wall,
I pluck you out of the crannies.
Hold you here, root and all, in my hand,
Little flower. But if I could understand
What you are, root and all, and all in all,
I should know what God and man is.

———

WILD flowers — I love them more than garden
      flowers, that seem at most
Sweet guests, or foreign cousins not half-speaking
The language of the land.

THE POWER IN DARKNESS.

That which we dare invoke to bless;
    Our dearest faith; our ghastliest doubt;
    He, They, One, All; within, without;
The Power in darkness whom we guess.

I found Him not in world, or sun,
    Or eagle's wing, or insect's eye:
    Nor through the questions men may try,
The petty cobwebs we have spun:

If e'er when faith had fallen asleep
    I heard a voice, "Believe no more,"
    And heard an ever-breaking shore
That tumbled in the Godless deep;

A warmth within the breast would melt
    The freezing reason's colder part,
    And like a man in wrath the heart
Stood up and answered, " I have felt."

No, like a child in doubt and fear:
    But that blind clamor made me wise:
    Then was I as a child that cries,
But, crying, knows his father near.

And what I seem beheld again
  What is, and no man understands;
  And out of darkness came the hands
That reach through Nature, moulding men.

VASTNESS.

Spring and Summer and Autumn and Winter,
  and all these old revolutions of earth;
All new-old revolutions of Empire — change of
  the tide, what is it all worth?

What the philosophies, all the sciences, poesy,
  varying voices of prayer?
All that is noblest, all that is basest, all that is
  filthy with all that is fair?

What is it all, if we all of us end but in being
  our own corpse-coffins at last,
Swallow'd in Vastness, lost in silence, drown'd
  in the deeps of a meaningless Past?

What but a murmur of gnats in the gloom, or a
  moment's anger of bees in their hive? •

.   •   •   •   •   •   •   •   •

Peace, let it be! for I loved him, and love him
  forever; the dead are not dead, but alive.

BIRTHDAY THOUGHTS.

Iᴛ is my birthday.
.   .   .   .   .   .   My mother,
For whose sake, and the blessed Queen of Heaven,
I reverence all women, bade me, dying,
Whene'er this day should come about, to carve
One lone hour from it, so to meditate
Upon my greater nearness to the birthday
Of the after-life, when all the sheeted dead
Are shaken from their stillness in the grave
By the last trumpet.

HUMILITY.

O, sᴏɴ! thou hast not true humility,
The highest virtue, mother of them all;
For when the Lord of all things made Himself
Naked of glory for His mortal change,
"Take thou my robe," she said, "for all is
        thine,"
And all her form shone forth with sudden light,
So that the angels were amazed, and she
Follow'd Him down, and like a flying star
Led on the gray-hair'd wisdom of the East,
But her thou hast not known; for what is this

Thou thoughtest of thy prowess and thy sins?
Thou hast not lost thyself to save thyself.

———

    NEVER yet
Could all of true and noble in knight and man
Twine round one sin, whatever it might be,
With such a closeness, but apart there grew
— Save that he were the swine thou spakest
      of —
Some root of knighthood and pure nobleness;
Whereto see thou, that it may bear its flower.

———

LET THERE BE LIGHT.

          To your question now,
Which touches on the workman and his work.
Let there be light, and there was light; 'tis so:
For was, and is, and will be, are but is;
And all creation is one act at once,
The birth of light; but we that are not all,
As parts, can see but parts, now this, now that,
And live, perforce, from thought to thought, and
      make
One act a phantom of succession: thus
Our weakness somehow shapes the shadow Time;
But in the shadow will we work. . . .

ASPIRATIONS.

I YEARN to breathe the airs of heaven
　　That often meet me here.
I muse on joy that will not cease,
　　Pure spaces clothed in living beams,
Pure lilies of eternal peace,
　　Whose odors haunt my dreams;
And, stricken by an angel's hand,
　　This mortal armor that I wear,
This weight and size, this heart and eyes
　　Are touched, are turned to finest air.
The clouds are broken in the sky,
　　And through the mountain-walls
A rolling organ-harmony
　　Swells up and shakes and falls,
Then moves the trees, the copses nod,
　　Wings flutter, voices hover clear:
O, just and faithful knight of God!
　　Ride on! the prize is near!

———

I CANNOT laud this life, it looks so dark,
　— dream of a shadow, go —
God bless you.　I shall join you in a day.

TRUST.

He as a brave God-fearing man
Bow'd himself down, and in that mystery
Where God-in-man is one with man-in-God,
Pray'd for a blessing on his wife and babes.

If you fear
Cast all your cares on God; that anchor holds.

Had not his poor heart
Spoken with That, which being everywhere
Lets none, who speaks with Him seem all alone,
Surely the man had died of solitude.

TEARS.

" Tears, idle tears, I know not what they mean,
Tears from the depth of some divine despair
Rise in the heart, and gather to the eyes,
In looking on the happy Autumn-fields
And thinking of the days that are no more.

" Fresh as the first beam glittering on a sail,
That brings our friends up from the underworld,
Sad as the last which reddens over one

That sinks with all we love below the verge;
So sad, so fresh, the days that are no more.

" Ah, sad and strange, as in dark summer dawns
The earliest pipe of half-awaken'd birds
To dying ears, when unto dying eyes
The casement slowly grows a glimmering square;
So sad, so strange, the days that are no more.

" Dear as remember'd kisses after death,
And sweet as those by hopeless fancy feign'd
On lips that are for others; deep as love,
Deep as first love, and wild with all regret;
O, Death in Life, the days that are no more."

―――

Come, Time, and teach me many years
   I do not suffer in a dream;
   For now so strange do these things seem,
Mine eyes have leisure for their tears.

―――

STEPPING-STONES.

I held it truth, with him who sings
   To one clear harp in divers tones,
   That men may rise on stepping-stones
Of their dead selves to higher things.

But who shall so forecast the years
    And find in loss a gain to match ?
    Or reach a hand through time to catch
The far-off interest of tears ?

Let Love clasp Grief, lest both be drown'd,
    Let darkness keep her raven gloss :
    Ah ! sweeter to be drunk with loss,
To dance with death, to beat the ground,

Than that the victor Hours should scorn
    The long result of love, and boast :
    "Behold the man that loved and lost,
But all he was is overworn."

GOOD-NIGHT SONG.

To sleep ! to sleep ! The long bright day is done,
And darkness rises from the fallen sun.
To sleep ! to sleep !
Whate'er thy joys, they vanish with the day ;
Whate'er thy griefs, in sleep they fade away.
To sleep ! to sleep !
Sleep, mournful heart, and let the past be past !
Sleep, happy soul ! all life will sleep at last.
To sleep ! to sleep !

THANKFULNESS.

For me, I thank the saints I am not great,
For if there ever come a grief to me,
I cry my cry in silence, and have done.
None knows it, and my tears have brought me
            good:
But even were the griefs of little ones
As great as those of great ones, yet this grief
Is added to the griefs the great must bear,
That howsoever much they may desire
Silence, they cannot weep behind a cloud.

LATE, SO LATE.

Late, late, so late! and dark the night and chill!
Late, late, so late! but we can enter still.
Too late, too late! ye cannot enter now.

No light had we; for that we do repent;
And hearing this the Bridegroom will relent.
Too late, too late! ye cannot enter now.

No light; so late! and dark and chill the night.
Oh! let us in, that we may find the light!
Too late, too late! ye cannot enter now.

Have we not heard the Bridegroom is so sweet?
O, let us in, though late, to kiss his feet!
No, no, too late! ye cannot enter now.

THE sin that practice burns into the blood,
And not the one dark hour which brings remorse
Will brand us, after, of whose fold we be.

DOUBT.

IT is a man's privilege to doubt,
If so be that from doubt at length
Truth may stand forth unmoved of change,
An image with profulgent brows
And perfect limbs, as from the storm
Of running fires and fluid range
Of lawless airs, at last stood out
This excellence and solid form
Of constant beauty.

SHALL we not look into the laws
Of life and death, and things that seem
And things that be, and analyze
Our double nature, and compare
All creeds till we have found the one,
If one there be? Ay me! I fear

All may not doubt, but everywhere
Some must clasp Idols.   Yet, my God,
Whom call I Idol?   Let Thy dove
Shadow me over, and my sins
Be unremember'd, and Thy love
Enlighten me.   Oh ! teach me yet
Somewhat before the heavy clod
Weighs on me, and the busy fret
Of that sharp-headed worm begins
In the gross blackness underneath.

———

LOVE.

Love that hath us in the net,
Can he pass, and we forget?
Many suns arise and set.
Many a chance the years beget.
Love the gift is Love the debt,
    Even so.

Love is hurt with jar and fret,
Love is made a vague regret.
Eyes with idle tears are wet,
Idle habit links us yet.
What is love ?   For we forget.
    Ah, no, no !

THE HOSPITAL.

Everywhere
Low voices with the ministering hand
Hung round the sick. The maidens came, they
    talked,
They sang, they read : till she not fair, began
To gather light, and she that was, became
Her former beauty treble ; and to and fro
With books, with flowers, and angel offices,
Like creatures native unto gracious act,
And in their own clear element, they moved.

FAME.

"Man dreams of Fame, while woman
   .   .   .   .   wakes to Love."
   .   .   .   .   Fame with men,
Being but ampler means to serve mankind,
Should have small rest or pleasure in herself,
But work as vassal to the larger love,
That dwarfs the petty love of one to one.
Use gave me Fame at first, and Fame again
Increasing gave me use.   Lo, these my boon !

He is all fault who hath no fault at all.

WAGES.

Glory of warrior, glory of orator, glory of song,
  Paid with a voice flying to be lost on an
    endless sea —
Glory of Virtue, to fight, to struggle, to right
    the wrong —
  Nay, but she aim'd not at glory, no lover of
    glory she :
  Give her the glory of going on, and still to be.

The wages of sin is death: if the wages of Vir-
    tue be dust,
  Would she have heart to endure for the life
    of the worm and the fly ?
She desires no isles of the blest, no quiet seats
    of the just,
  To rest in a golden grove, or to bask in a
    summer sky ;
  Give her the wages of going on, and not to die.

TRUTH.

Though truths in manhood darkly join,
  Deep-seated in our mystic frame,
  We yield all blessings to the name
Of Him that made them current coin.

For wisdom dealt with mortal powers,
  Where Truth in closest words shall fail,
  When Truth embodied in a tale
Shall enter in at lowly doors.

And so the Word had breath, and wrought
  With human hands the creed of creeds
  In loveliness of perfect deeds,
More strong than all poetic thought.

FORTUNE AND HER WHEEL.

Turn, Fortune, turn thy wheel and lower the
    proud;
Turn thy wild wheel through sunshine, storm
    and cloud;
Thy wheel and thee we neither love nor hate.

Turn, Fortune, turn thy wheel with smile or
    frown;
With that wild wheel we go not up or down;
Our hoard is little, but our hearts are great.

Smite and we smile, the lords of many lands,
Frown and we smile, the lords of our own hands;
For man is man and master of his fate.

Turn, turn thy wheel above the staring crowd;
Thy wheel and thou art shadows in the cloud;
Thy wheel and thee we neither love nor hate.

――――

TRUST IN LOVE.

"In Love, if Love be Love, if Love be ours,
Faith and unfaith can ne'er be equal powers;
Unfaith in aught is want of faith in all.

"It is the little rift within the lute,
That by and by will make the music mute,
And ever widening slowly silence all.

"The little rift within the lover's lute,
Or little pitted speck in garnered fruit,
That rotting inward slowly moulders all.

"It is not worth the keeping; let it go;
But shall it?   Answer, darling, answer no,
And trust me not at all, or all in all."

――――

What delights can equal those
   That stir the spirit's inner deeps,
   When one that loves, but knows not, reaps
A truth from one that loves and knows?

THE FLOWER.

ONCE in a golden hour
  I cast to earth a seed,
Up there came a flower,
  The people said, a weed.

To and fro they went
  Thro' my garden-bower,
And muttering discontent
  Cursed me and my flower.

Then it grew so tall
  It wore a crown of light,
But thieves from o'er the wall
  Stole the seed by night.

Sow'd it far and wide
  By every town and tower,
Till all the people cried,
  " Splendid is the flower ! "

Read my little fable :
  He that runs may read,
Most can raise the flowers now,
  For all have got the seed.

And some are pretty enough,
    And some are poor indeed;
And now again the people
    Call it but a weed.

WORDS.

I SOMETIMES hold it half a sin
    To put in words the grief I feel,
    For words, like nature, half reveal
And half conceal the Soul within.

But, for the unquiet heart and brain,
    A use in measured language lies;
    The sad mechanic exercise,
Like dull narcotics, numbing pain.

AN ALLEGORY.

I SEND you a sort of allegory
(For you will understand) of a soul,
A sinful soul possessed of many gifts,
A spacious garden full of flowering weeds,
A glorious Devil, large in heart and brain,
That did love Beauty only (Beauty seen
In all varieties of mold and mind),
And Knowledge for its beauty: or if Good,

Good only for its beauty, seeing not
That Beauty, Good and Knowledge are three
    sisters
That dote upon each other, friends to man,
Living together under the same roof,
And never can be sundered without tears.
And he that shuts Love out, in turn shall be
Shut out from Love, and on her threshold lie
Howling in outer darkness. Not for this
Was common clay ta'en from the common
    earth,
Moulded by God, and tempered with the tears
Of angels to the perfect shape of men.

A LOVE SONG.

Go not, happy day,
  From the shining fields,
Go not, happy day,
  Till the maiden yields.
Rosy is the West,
  Rosy is the South,
Roses are her cheeks,
  And a rose her mouth.
When the happy Yes
  Falters from her lips,

Pass and blush the news
　　O'er the blowing ships,
Over blowing seas,
　　Over seas at rest,
Pass the happy news,
　　Blush it thro' the West;
Till the red man dance
　　By his red cedar-tree,
And the red man's babe
　　Leap, beyond the sea.
Blush from West to East,
　　Blush from East to West,
Till the West is East,
　　Blush it thro' the West.
Rosy is the West,
　　Rosy is the South,
Roses are her cheeks,
　　And a rose her mouth.

THE OAK.

Live thy life,
　　Young and old,
Like yon oak,
Bright in spring,
　　Living gold.

Summer — rich
    Then ; and then
Autumn — changed,
Soberer-hued,
    Gold again.

All his leaves
    Fall'n at length,
Look, he stands,
Trunk and bough,
    Naked strength.

———

IF Nature put not forth her power
About the opening of the flower,
Who is it that could live an hour ?

———

O LIVING WILL!

O LIVING will that shalt endure
    When all that seems shall suffer shock,
    Rise in the spiritual rock,
Flow through our deeds and make them pure,

That we may lift from out the dust
    A voice as unto him that hears
    A cry above the conquered years
To one that with us works and trusts.

With faith that comes of self-control,
  The truths that never can be proved
  Until we close with all we loved,
And all we flow from, soul in soul.

———

PROGRESS.

" 'Twere better not to breathe or speak,
Than cry for strength, remaining weak,
And seem to find, but still to seek.

. . . .

" Cry, faint not, climb.

. . . .

" Sometimes a little corner shines,
As over rainy mist inclines
A gleaming crag with belts of pines.

. . . .

  .   .   .   " Some have striven
Achieving calm, to whom was given
The joy that mixes man with Heaven.

" Who, rowing hard against the stream,
Saw distant gates of Eden gleam,
And did not dream it was a dream;

" But heard, by secret transport led,
Even in the charnels of the dead,
The murmur of the fountain-head —

Which did accomplish their desire,
Bore and forbore, and did not tire,
Like Stephen, an unquenched fire.

He heeded not reviling tones.
.   .   .   .
But looking upward, full of grace,
He prayed, and from a happy place
God's glory smote him on the face.

FORGIVENESS.

"FORGIVE! How many will say 'forgive' and
    find
A sort of absolution in the sound
To hate a little longer!"

       SHE kept a tender Christian hope
Haunting a holy text, and still to that
Returning, as the bird returns, at night,
" Let not the sun go down upon your wrath,"
Said, "Love, forgive him :" but he did not speak,
And silenced by that silence lay the wife,
Remembering her dear Lord who died for all,
And musing on the little lives of men,
And how they mar this little by their feuds.

THE TRIUMPH OF LOVE.

Love took up the glass of Time, and turn'd it
    in his glowing hands ;
Every moment, lightly shaken, ran itself in
    golden sands.

Love took up the harp of Life, and smote on all
    the chords with might ;
Smote the chord of Self, that, trembling, pass'd
    in music out of sight.

———

Love is love for evermore.

———

TRUE AND FALSE.

O purblind race of miserable men,
How many among us at this very hour
Do forge a life-long trouble for ourselves,
By taking true for false, or false for true :
Here, through the feeble twilight of this world
Groping, how many, until we pass and reach
That other, where we see as we are seen !

———

Sin is too dull to see beyond himself.

FROM THE LOTOS-EATERS.

THERE is sweet music here that softer falls
Than petals from blown roses on the grass,
Or night-dews on still waters between walls
Of shadowy granite, in a gleaming pass;
Music that gentlier on the spirit lies,
Than tir'd eyelids upon tir'd eyes:
Music that brings sweet sleep down from the
    blissful skies.
Here are cool mosses deep,
And thro' the moss the ivies creep,
And in the stream the long-leaved flowers weep,
And from the craggy ledge the poppy hangs in
    sleep.

.   .   .   .

Lo! in the middle of the wood,
The folded leaf is woo'd from out the bud
With winds upon the branch, and there
Grows green and broad, and takes no care,
Sun-steep'd at noon, and in the moon
Nightly dew-fed; and turning yellow
Falls, and floats adown the air.
Lo! sweeten'd with the summer light,
The full-juiced apple, waxing over-mellow,
Drops in a silent autumn night.

All its allotted length of days,
The flower ripens in its place,
Ripens, and fades, and falls, and hath no toil,
Fast-rooted in the fruitful soil.

THE SHELL.

I.

SEE what a lovely shell,
Small and pure as a pearl,
Lying close to my foot,
Frail, but a work divine,
Made so fairily well
With delicate spire and whorl,
How exquisitely minute,
A miracle of design !

II.

What is it ? a learned man
Could give it a clumsy name.
Let him name it who can,   .
The beauty would be the same.

III.

The tiny cell is forlorn,
Void of the little living will

That made it stir on the shore.
Did he stand at the diamond door
Of his house in a rainbow frill ?
Did he push, when he was uncurl'd,
A golden foot, or a fairy horn
Thro' his dim water-world ?

iv.

Slight, to be crush'd with a tap
Of my finger-nail on the sand,
Small, but a work divine,
Frail, but of force to withstand,
Year upon year, the shock
Of cataract seas that snap
The three-decker's oaken spine
Athwart the ledges of rock.

.   .   .   .

———

Doth not the fewness of anything make the fullness of it in estimation ?

———

STEADFAST LOVE.

Forget him — never .   .   .   .
.   .   .   Never !
Not while the swallow skims along the ground,
And while the lark flies up and touches heaven !

Not while the smoke floats from the cottage
  roof,
And the white cloud is roll'd along the sky!
Not while the rivulet babbles by the door,
And the great breaker beats upon the beach!
Never!
Till nature, high and low, and great and small
Forgets herself, and all her loves and hates
Sink again into chaos.

TITHONUS.

THE woods decay, the woods decay and fall,   .
The vapors weep their burthen to the ground,
Man comes and tills the field and lies beneath,
And after many a summer dies the swan.
Me only cruel immortality
Consumes : I wither slowly in thine arms,
Here at the quiet limit of the world,
A white-hair'd shadow roaming like a dream
The ever silent spaces of the East,
Far-folded mists, and gleaming halls of morn.
 Alas ! for this gray shadow, once a man —
So glorious in his beauty and thy choice,
Who madest him thy chosen, that he seem'd
To his great heart none other than a God !

I ask'd thee, " Give me immortality."
Then didst thou grant mine asking with a
    smile,
Like wealthy men who care not how they give.
But thy strong Hours indignant work'd their
    wills,
And beat me down, and marr'd and wasted
    me,
And tho' they could not end me, left me maim'd
To dwell in presence of immortal youth,
Immortal age beside immortal youth,
And all I was, in ashes. Can thy love,
Thy beauty, make amends, tho' even now,
Close over us, the silver star, thy guide,
Shines in those tremulous eyes that fill with
    tears
To hear me ? Let me go : take back thy gift:
Why should a man desire in any way
To vary from the kindly race of men,
Or pass beyond the goal of ordinance
Where all should pause, as is most meet for all ?

A soft air fans the cloud apart : there comes
A glimpse of that dark world where I was
    born.
Once more the old mysterious glimmer steals

From thy pure brows, and from thy shoulders
      pure,
And bosom beating with a heart renew'd.
Thy cheek begins to redden thro' the gloom,
Thy sweet eyes brighten slowly close to mine,
Ere yet they blind the stars, and the wild team
Which love thee, yearning for thy yoke, arise,
And shake the darkness from their loosen'd
      manes,
And beat the twilight into flakes of fire.

Lo ! ever thus thou growest beautiful
In silence, then before thine answer given
Departest, and thy tears are on my cheek.

Why wilt thou ever scare me with thy tears,
And make me tremble lest a saying learnt
In days far-off, on that dark earth be true ?
" The Gods themselves cannot recall their
      gifts."

Ay me ! ay me ! with what another heart
In days far-off, and with what other eyes
I used to watch — if I be he that watch'd —
The lucid outline forming round thee ; saw
The dim curls kindle into sunny rings ;

Changed with thy mystic change, and felt my
 blood
Glow with the glow that slowly crimson'd all
Thy presence and thy portals, while I lay,
Mouth, forehead, eyelids, growing dewy-warm
With kisses balmier than half-opening buds
Of April, and could hear the lips that kiss'd
Whispering I knew not what of wild and sweet,
Like that strange song I heard Apollo sing,
While Ilion like a mist rose into towers.

Yet hold me not forever in thine East:
How can my nature longer mix with thine?
Coldly thy rosy shadows bathe me, cold
Are all thy lights, and cold my wrinkled feet
Upon thy glimmering thresholds, when the
 steam
Floats up from those dim fields about the homes
Of happy men that have the power to die,
And grassy barrows of the happier dead.
Release me, and restore me to the ground:
Thou seëst all things, thou wilt see my grave;
Thou wilt renew thy beauty morn by morn;
I earth in earth forget these empty courts,
And thee returning on thy silver wheels.

THE HIGHER PANTHEISM.

THE sun, the moon, the stars, the seas, the hills
    and the plains —
Are not these, O Soul, the Vision of Him who
    reigns ?

Is not the Vision He ? tho' He be not that
    which He seems ?
Dreams are true while they last, and do we not
    live in dreams ?

Earth, these solid stars, this weight of body and
    limb,
Are they not sign and symbol of thy division
    from Him ?

Dark is the world to thee : thyself art the reason
    why ;
For is He not all but thou, that hast power to
    feel "I am I ! "

Glory about thee, without thee : and thou ful-
    fillest thy doom.
Making Him broken gleams, and a stifled splen-
    dor and gloom.

Speak to Him thou for He hears, and Spirit
   with Spirit can meet —
Closer is He than breathing, and nearer than
   hands and feet.

God is law, say the wise, O Soul, and let us
   rejoice,
For if He thunder by law, the thunder is yet
   His voice.

Law is God, say some : no God at all, says the
   fool ;
For all we have power to see is a straight staff
   bent in a pool ;

And the ear of man cannot hear, and the eye of
   man cannot see ;
But if we could see and hear, this Vision — were
   it not He ?

ONWARD.

Deliver not the tasks of might
   To weakness, neither hide the ray
   From those, not blind, who wait for day,
Tho' sitting girt with doubtful light.

Make knowledge circle with the winds;
   But let her herald, Reverence, fly
   Before her to whatever sky;
Bear seed of men and growth of minds.

Watch what main-currents draw the years:
   Cut Prejudice against the grain:
   But gentle words are always gain,
Regard the weakness of thy peers.

Nor toil for title, place or touch
   Of pension, neither count on praise;
   It grows to guerdon after-days;
Nor deal in watch-words overmuch.

Not clinging to some ancient saw;
   Nor master'd by some modern term;
   Not swift but slow to change, but firm;
And in its season bring the law;

That from Discussion's lips may fall
   With Life, that, working, strongly binds —
   Set all in lights by many minds
To close the interest of all.

THE EAGLE.

He clasps the crag with hooked hands ;
Close to the sun in lonely lands,
Ring'd with the azure world, he stands,
The wrinkled sea beneath him crawls ;
He watches from his mountain walls,
And like a thunderbolt he falls.

BROTHERHOOD.

Let the fair white-wing'd peacemaker fly
To happy havens under the sky,
And mix the seasons, and the golden hours ;
Till each man finds his own in all men's good,
And all men work in noble brotherhood
Breaking their mailèd fleets and armèd towers,
And ruling by obeying Nature's powers,
And gathering all the fruits of earth and crown'd
    with all her flowers.

FAITH.

His resolve
Upbore him, and firm faith, and evermore
Prayer from a living source within the will,
And beating up thro' all the bitter world,

Like fountains of sweet water in the sea,
Kept him a living soul.

———

AND all is well, though faith and form
 Be sundered in the night of fear:
 Well roars the storm to those that hear
A deeper voice across the storm.

———

THE BROOK.

  "O, brook," he says,
"O, babbling brook, whence come you?"
And the brook, why not? replies,

I come from haunts of coot and hern,
 I make a sudden sally
And sparkle out among the fern,
 To bicker down a valley.

By thirty hills I hurry down,
 Or slip between the ridges,
By twenty thorps, a little town,
 And half a hundred bridges.

I chatter over stony ways,
 In little sharps and trebles,

I bubble into eddying bays,
 I babble on the pebbles.

With many a curve my banks I fret
 By many a field and fallow,
And many a fairy foreland set
 With willow-weed and mallow.

I chatter, chatter, as I flow
 To join the brimming river,
For men may come and men may go,
 But I go on forever.

I wind about, and in and out,
 With here a blossom sailing,
And here and there a lusty trout,
 And here and there a grayling,

And here and there a foamy flake
 Upon me, as I travel,
With many a silvery waterbreak
 Above the golden gravel,

And draw them all along, and flow
 To join the brimming river,
For men may come and men may go,
 But I go on forever.

I steal by lawns and grassy plots,
    I slide by hazel covers ;
I move the sweet forget-me-nots
    That grow for happy lovers.

I slip, I slide, I gloom, I glance,
    Among my skimming swallows ;
I make the netted sunbeam dance
    Against my sandy shallows.

I murmur under moon and stars
    In brambly wildernesses ;
I linger by my shingly bars ;
    I loiter round my cresses ;

And out again I curve and flow
    To join the brimming river,
For men may come and men may go,
    But I go on for ever.

IN THE CHILDREN'S HOSPITAL.

I.

Our doctor had call'd in another, I never had
    seen him before,
But he sent a chill to my heart when I saw him
    come in at the door,

Fresh from the surgery-schools of France and
of other lands —
Harsh red hair, big voice, big chest, big merci-
less hands !
Wonderful cures he had done, O yes ! but they
said too of him
He was happier using the knife than in trying
to save the limb,
And that I can well believe, for he look'd so
coarse and red,
I could think he was one of those who would
break their jests on the dead,
And mangle the living dog that had loved him
and fawn'd at his knee —
Drench'd with the hellish oorali — that ever
such things should be !

II.

Here was a boy — I am sure that some of our
children would die
But for the voice of Love, and the smile, and
the comforting eye —
Here was a boy in the ward, every bone seem'd
out of its place —
Caught in a mill and crush'd — it was all but a
hopeless case :

And he handled him gently enough; but his
    voice and his face were not kind,
And it was but a hopeless case, he had seen it
    and made up his mind,
And he said to me roughly, "The lad will need
    little more of your care."
"All the more need," I told him, "to seek the
    Lord Jesus in prayer;
They are all his children here, and I pray for
    them all as my own;"
But he turn'd to me, "Ay, good woman, can
    prayer set a broken bone?"
Then he mutter'd half to himself, but I know
    that I heard him say,
"All very well — but the good Lord Jesus has
    had his day."

III.

Had? has it come? It has only dawn'd. It
    will come by and by.
O how could I serve in the wards if the hope of
    the world were a lie?
How could I bear with the sights and the loath-
    some smells of disease,
But that He said, "Ye do it to me, when ye do
    it to these?"

IV.

So he went.   And we past to this ward where
    the younger children are laid :
Here is the cot of our orphan, our darling, our
    meek little maid ;
Empty you see just now ! We have lost her
    who loved her so much —
Patient of pain tho' as quick as a sensitive plant
    to the touch;
Hers was the prettiest prattle, it often moved
    me to tears,
Hers was the gratefullest heart I have found in
    a child of her years —
Nay, you remember our Emmie ; you used to
    send her the flowers ;
How she would smile at 'em, play with 'em,
    talk to 'em hours after hours !
They that can wander at will where the works
    of the Lord are reveal'd
Little guess what joy can be got from a cowslip
    out of the field ;
Flowers to these " spirits in prison " are all
    they can know of the spring,
They freshen and sweeten the wards like the
    waft of an Angel's wing ;

And she lay with a flower in one hand and her
    thin hands crost on her breast —
Wan, but as pretty as heart can desire, and we
    thought her at rest,
Quietly sleeping — so quiet, our doctor said
    "Poor little dear,
Nurse, I must do it to-morrow; she'll never live
    thro' it, I fear."

v.

I walk'd with our kindly old doctor as far as
    the head of the stair,
Then I return'd to the ward; the child didn't
    see I was there.

vi.

Never since I was a nurse, had I been so grieved
    and so vext!
Emmie had heard him. Softly she call'd from
    her cot to the next,
"He says I shall never live thro' it, O Annie,
    what shall I do?"
Annie consider'd, "If I," said the wise little
    Annie, "was you,
I should cry to the dear Lord Jesus to help me,
    for, Emmie, you see,

It's all in the picture there : ' Little children
    should come to me.' "
(Meaning the print that you gave us, I find that
    it always can please
Our children, the dear Lord Jesus with children
    about his knees.)
" Yes, and I will," said Emmie, " but then if I
    call to the Lord,
How should He know that it's me ? such a lot
    of beds in the ward ! "
That was a puzzle for Annie. Again she con-
    sider'd and said :
"Emmie, you put out your arms, and you leave
    'em outside on the bed —
The Lord has so much to see to ! but, Emmie,
    you tell it Him plain,
It's the little girl with her arms lying out on
    the counterpane."

VII.

I had sat three nights by the child — I could
    not watch her for four —
My brain had begun to reel — I felt I could do
    it no more.
That was my sleeping night, but I thought that
    it never would pass,

There was a thunder-clap once, and a clatter of
    hail on the glass,
And there was a phantom cry that I heard as I
    tost about,
The motherless bleat of a lamb in the storm and
    the darkness without;
My sleep was broken besides with dreams of
    the dreadful knife
And fears for our delicate Emmie who scarce
    would escape with her life;
Then in the gray of the morning it seem'd she
    stood by me and smiled,
And the doctor came at his hour, and we went
    to see the child.

VIII.

He had brought his ghastly tools: we believed
    her asleep again —
Her dear, long, lean, little arms lying out on
    the counterpane ;
Say that His day is done! Ah why should we
    care what they say ?
The Lord of the children had heard her, and
    Emmie had past away.

A SECOND VOICE.

A SECOND voice was at mine ear,
A little whisper silver-clear,
A murmur, "Be of better cheer."

As from some blissful neighborhood,
A notice faintly understood,
"I see the end, and know the good."

A little hint to solace woe,
A hint, a whisper breathing low,
"I may not speak of what I know."

Like an Æolian harp that wakes
No certain air, but overtakes
Far thought with music that it makes:

Such seem'd the whisper at my side,
"What is it thou knowest, sweet voice?" I
    cried.
"A hidden hope," the voice replied.

So heavenly-toned, that in that hour
From out my sullen heart a power
Broke, like the rainbow from the shower,

To feel, altho' no tongue can prove,
That every cloud that spreads above
And veileth love, itself is love.

And forth into the fields I went,
And Nature's living motion lent
The pulse of hope to discontent.

I wonder'd at the bounteous hours,
The slow result of winter showers:
You scarce could see the grass for flowers.

I wonder'd while I paced along:
The woods were fill'd so full with song,
There seem'd no room for sense of wrong;

And all so variously wrought.
I marvel'd how the mind was brought
To anchor by one gloomy thought;

And wherefore rather I made choice
To commune with a barren voice,
Than him that said "Rejoice! rejoice!"

Part Second.

———

MEN AND WOMEN.

MEN AND WOMEN.

THE woman's cause is man's; they rise or sink
Together, dwarfed or godlike, bond or free,
For she that out of Lethe scales with man
The shining steps of Nature, shares with man
His nights, his days, moves with him to one
  goal,
Stays all the fair young planet in her hands —
If she be small, slight-natured, miserable,
How shall men grow ?

———

WOMAN is not undeveloped man,
But diverse ; could we make her as the man,
Sweet love were slain, whose dearest bond is this :
Not like . . but like in difference :
Yet in the long years liker must they grow ;
The man be more of woman, she of man ;
He gain in sweetness and in moral height,
Nor lose the wrestling thews that throw the
  world ;
She mental breadth, nor fail in childward care ;
More as the double-natured Poet each :

Till at the last she set herself to man,
Like perfect music unto noble words;
And so these twain, upon the skirts of Time,
Sit side by side, full-summed in all their powers
Dispensing harvest, sowing the To-be,
Self-reverent each and reverencing each,
Distinct in individualities,
But like each other even as those who love.
Then comes the statelier Eden back to men;
Then reign the world's great bridals, chaste and
    calm;
Then springs the crowning race of humankind.
May these things be !

———

                   EITHER sex alone
Is half itself, and in true marriage lies
Nor equal, nor unequal : each fulfills
Defect in each, and always thought in thought,
Purpose in purpose, will in will, they grow,
The single pure and perfect animal,
The two-celled heart, beating with one full stroke
Life.

———

             FROM earlier than I know,
Immersed in rich foreshadowing of the world,
I loved the woman: . . .

. . . .   There was one through whom I loved
      her, one
Not learned, save in gracious household ways,
Not perfect, nay, but full of tender wants,
No Angel, but a dearer being, all dipt
In Angel instincts, breathing Paradise,
Interpreter between the gods and men,
Who looked all native to her place, and yet
On tiptoe seemed to touch upon a sphere
Too gross to tread, and all male minds perforce
Swayed to her from their orbits as they moved
And girdled her with music. Happy he
With such a mother! faith in womankind
Beats with his blood, and trust in all things high
Comes easy to him, and though he trip and fall,
He shall not blind his soul with clay.

———

When the man wants weight the woman takes
      it up,
And topples down the scales ; but this is fixt
As are the roots of earth and base of all.
Man for the field, and woman for the hearth :
Man for the sword, and for the needle she :
Man with the head, and woman with the heart :
Man to command, and woman to obey.

> My bride,
> My wife, my life, Oh! we will walk this world,
> Yoked in all exercise of noble end.

> THE bearing and the training of a child
> Is woman's wisdom.

THE ORDER OF THE ROUND TABLE.

A GLORIOUS company, the flower of men,
To serve as models for the mighty world.
.　　.　　.　　.　　.　　.　　.　　.　　.
I made them lay their hands in mine and swear
To reverence the King, as if he were
Their conscience, and their conscience as their
　　　King,
To break the heathen and uphold the Christ,
To ride abroad redressing human wrongs,
To speak no slander, no, nor listen to it,
To lead sweet lives in purest chastity,
To love one maiden only, cleave to her,
And worship her by years of noble deeds,
Until they won her: for indeed I knew
Of no more subtle master under heaven
Than is the maiden passion for a maid
Not only to keep down the base in man,

But teach high thought, and amiable words,
And courtliness, and the desire of fame,
And a love of truth, and all that makes a man.

ADELINE.

Mystery of mysteries,
  Faintly smiling Adeline,
    Scarce of earth nor all divine,
      Nor unhappy, nor at rest,
        But beyond expression fair.
        With thy floating flaxen hair;
Thy rose-lips and full blue eyes
      Take the heart from out my breast.
Wherefore those dim looks of thine,
Shadowy, dreaming Adeline?

Whence that aery bloom of thine,
  Like a lily which the sun
Looks thro' in his sad decline,
  And a rose-bush leans upon,
Thou that faintly smilest still,
  As a Naiad in a well,
  Looking at the set of day,
Or a phantom two hours old
  Of a maiden past away,

Ere the placid lips be cold?
Wherefore those faint smiles of thine,
  Spiritual Adeline?

What hope or fear or joy is thine?
Who talketh with thee, Adeline?
  For sure thou art not all alone:
    Do beating hearts of salient springs
  Keep measure with thine own?
      Hast thou heard the butterflies
    What they say betwixt their wings?
    Or in stillest evenings
With what voice the violet woos
To his heart the silver dews?
    Or when little airs arise,
    How the merry bluebell rings
      To the mosses underneath?
      Hast thou look'd upon the breath
    Of the lilies at sunrise?
Wherefore that faint smile of thine,
Shadowy, dreaming Adeline?

Some honey-converse feeds thy mind,
  Some spirit of a crimson rose
  In love with thee forgets to close
  His curtains, wasting odorous sighs

All night long on darkness blind.
What aileth thee ? whom waitest thou
With thy soften'd, shadow'd brow,
  And those dew-lit eyes of thine,
  Thou faint smiler, Adeline ?

Lovest thou the doleful wind
  When thou gazest at the skies ?
Doth the low-tongued Orient
  Wander from the side o' the morn,
    Dripping with Sabæan spice
On thy pillow, lowly bent
  With melodious airs lovelorn,
Breathing Light against thy face
While his locks a-dropping twined
  Round thy neck in subtle ring
Make a carcanet of rays,
  And ye talk together still,
  In the language wherewith Spring
  Letters cowslips on the hill ?
Hence that look and smile of thine,
  Spiritual Adeline.

ISABEL.

Eyes not down-dropt nor over-bright, but fed
With the clear-pointed flame of chastity,
Clear, without heat, undying, tended by
Pure vestal thoughts in the translucent fane
Of her still spirit; locks not wide dispread,
Madonna-wise on either side her head;
Sweet lips whereon perpetually did reign
The summer calm of golden charity,
Were fixed shadows of thy fixed mood,
Revered Isabel, the crown and head,
The stately flower of female fortitude,
Of perfect wifehood and pure lowlihead.

The intuitive decision of a bright
And thorough-edged intellect to part
Error from crime; a prudence to withhold;
The laws of marriage character'd in gold
Upon the blanched tablets of her heart;
A love still burning upward, giving light
To read those laws; an accent very low
In blandishment, but a most silver flow
Of subtle-paced counsel in distress,
Right to the heart and brain, tho' undescried,
Winning its way with extreme gentleness

Thro' all the outworks of suspicious pride;
A courage to endure and to obey;
A hate of gossip parlance and of sway,
Crown'd Isabel, thro' all her placid life,
The queen of marriage, a most perfect wife.

The mellow'd reflex of a winter moon;
A clear stream flowing with a muddy one,
Till in its onward current it absorbs
With swifter movement and in purer light
The vexed eddies of its wayward brother;
A leaning and upbearing parasite,
Clothing the stem, which else had fallen quite,
With cluster'd flower-bells and ambrosial orbs
Of rich fruit-bunches leaning on each other —
Shadow forth thee; — the world hath not an-
    other
(Tho' all her fairest forms are types of thee
And thou of God in thy great charity)
Of such a finish'd chasten'd purity.

———

    TRUE women . . .
That have as many differences as men . . .
 .   .   .   .
    The violet varies from the lily as far
As oak from elm.

MADELINE.

Thou art not steep'd in golden languors,
   No tranced summer calm is thine,
      Ever varying Madeline.
   Thro' light and shadow thou dost range,
   Sudden glances, sweet and strange,
Delicious spites and darling angers,
   And airy forms of flitting change.

Smiling, frowning, evermore,
Thou art perfect in love-lore.
Revealings deep and clear are thine
Of wealthy smiles ; but who may know
Whether smile or frown be fleeter ?
Whether smile or frown be sweeter,
      Who may know ?
Frowns perfect-sweet along the brow
Light-glooming over eyes divine,
Like little clouds, sun-fringed, are thine,
      Every varying Madeline.
   Thy smile and frown are not aloof
      From one another,
      Each to each is dearest brother ;
   Hues of the silken sheeny woof
      Momently shot into each other.

All the mystery is thine;
Smiling, frowning, evermore,
Thou art perfect in love-lore,
    Ever varying Madeline.

A subtle, sudden flame,
  By veering passion fann'd,
    About thee breaks and dances;
  When I would kiss thy hand,
The flush of anger'd shame
    O'erflows thy calmer glances,
And o'er black brows drops down
A sudden-curved frown.
But when I turn away,
Thou, willing me to stay,
  Wooest not, nor vainly wranglest;
    But, looking fixedly the while,
  All my bounding heart entanglest
    In a golden-netted smile;
Then in madness and in bliss,
If my lips should dare to kiss
Thy taper fingers amorously,
Again thou blushest angerly;
And o'er black brows drops down
A sudden-curved frown.

ROSALIND.

My Rosalind, my Rosalind,
My frolic falcon, with bright eyes,   [flight,
Whose free delight, from any height of rapid
Stoops at all game that wing the skies,
My Rosalind, my Rosalind,
My bright-eyed, wild-eyed falcon, whither,
Careless both of wind and weather,
Whither fly ye, what game spy ye,
Up or down the streaming wind ?

The quick lark's closest-caroll'd strains
The shadow rushing up the sea,
The lightning flash atween the rains,
The sunlight driving down the lea,
The leaping stream, the very wind,
That will not stay, upon his way,
To stoop the cowslip to the plains,
Is not so clear and bold and free
As you, my falcon Rosalind.
You care not for another's pains,
Because you are the soul of joy,
Bright metal all without alloy.
Life shoots and glances thro' your veins,
And flashes off a thousand ways,

Thro' lips and eyes in subtle rays.
Your hawk-eyes are keen and bright,
Keen with triumph, watching still
To pierce me thro' with pointed light,
But oftentimes they flash and glitter
Like sunshine on a dancing rill,
And your words are seeming-bitter,
Sharp and few, but seeming-bitter
From excess of swift delight.

Come down, come home, my Rosalind,
My gay young hawk, my Rosalind:
Too long you keep the upper skies;
Too long you roam and wheel at will;
But we must hood your random eyes
That care not whom they kill.
And your cheek, whose brilliant hue
Is so sparkling-fresh to view,
Some red heath-flower in the dew,
Touch'd with sunrise. We must bind
And keep you fast, my Rosalind,
Fast, fast, my wild-eyed Rosalind,
And clip your wings, and make you love:
When we have lured you from above,
And that delight of frolic flight, by day or night,
From North to South;

We'll bind you fast in silken cords
And kiss away the bitter words
From off your rosy mouth.

A MOTHER.

My Mother looked as whole as some serene
Creation united in the golden moods
Of Sovereign artists; not a thought, a touch,
But pure as lines of green that streak the white
Of the first snowdrop's inner leaves.

My Mother was as mild as any saint,
And nearly canonized by all she knew,
So gracious was her tact and tenderness.

THE GOOD OLD NAME.

   . . . HE joined
Each office of the social hour
To noble manners, as the flower
And native growth of noble mind;

Nor ever narrowness or spite
  O villain fancy fleeting by,
  Drew in the expression of an eye
Where God and Nature met in light.

And thus he bore without abuse,
   The grand old name of gentleman
   Defamed by every charlatan
And soiled with all ignoble use.

LILIAN.

   AIRY, fairy Lilian,
   Flitting, fairy Lilian,
When I ask her if she love me,
Claps her tiny hands above me,
   Laughing all she can ;
She'll not tell me if she love me,
   Cruel little Lilian.

   When my passion seeks
   Pleasance in love-sighs,
She, looking thro' and thro' me
Thoroughly to undo me,
   Smiling, never speaks :
So innocent-arch, so cunning-simple,
From beneath her gather'd wimple
   Glancing with black-beaded eyes,
Till the lightning laughters dimple
   The baby-roses in her cheeks ;
   Then away she flies.

Prithee weep, May Lilian!
   Gayety without eclipse
Wearieth me, May Lilian:
Thro' my very heart it thrilleth
   When from crimson-threaded lips
Silver-treble laughter trilleth:
   Prithee weep, May Lilian.

     Praying all I can,
  If prayers will not hush thee,
     Airy Lilian,
  Like a rose-leaf I will crush thee,
     Fairy Lilian.

ELEÄNORE.

Thy dark eyes open'd not,
Nor first reveal'd themselves to English air,
   For there is nothing here,
Which, from the outward to the inward brought,
Moulded thy baby thought.
Far off from human neighborhood,
   Thou wert born, on a summer morn,
A mile beneath the cedar-wood.
Thy bounteous forehead was not fann'd
   With breezes from our oaken glades,

But thou wert nursed in some delicious land
    Of lavish lights and floating shades :
And flattering thy childish thought,
    The oriental fairy brought,
      At the moment of thy birth,
From old well-heads of haunted rills,
And the heart of purple hills,
    And shadow'd coves on a sunny shore,
      The choicest wealth of all the earth,
    Jewel or shell, or starry ore,
    To deck thy cradle Eleänore.

.   .   .   .

How many full-sail'd verse express,
    How many measured words adore
      The full-flowing harmony
Of thy swan-like stateliness,
          Eleänore ?
    The luxuriant symmetry
Of thy floating gracefulness,
          Eleänore ?
    Every turn and glance of thine,
    Every lineament divine,
          Eleänore,
    And the steady sunset glow,
    That stays upon thee ?   For in thee

Is nothing sudden, nothing single :
Like two streams of incense free
   From one censer in one shrine,
Thought and motion mingle,
Mingle ever. Motions flow
To one another, even as tho'
They were modulated so
   To an unheard melody,
Which lives about thee, and a sweep
   Of richest pauses, evermore
Drawn from each other mellow-deep ;
   Who may express thee, Eleänore ?

I stand before thee, Eleänore ;
   I see thy beauty gradually unfold.
Daily and hourly, more and more.
I muse, as in a trance, the while
   Slowly, as from a cloud of gold,
Comes out thy deep ambrosial smile.
I muse, as in a trance, whene'er
   The languors of thy love-deep eyes
Float on to me. I would I were
   So tranced, so rapt in ecstasies,
To stand apart, and to adore,
Gazing on thee for evermore,
Serene, imperial Eleänore !

Sometimes, with most intensity
Gazing, I seem to see
Thought folded over thought, smiling asleep,
Slowly awaken'd, grow so full and deep
In thy large eyes, that, overpower'd quite,
I cannot veil, or droop my sight,
But am as nothing in its light :
As tho' a star, in inmost heaven set,
Ev'n while we gaze on it,
Should slowly round his orb, and slowly grow
To a full face, then like a sun remain
Fix'd—then as slowly fade again,
    And draw itself to what it was before ;
      So full, so deep, so slow,
      Thought seems to come and go
    In thy large eyes, imperial Eleänore.

As thunder-clouds, that hung on high,
    Roof'd the world with doubt and fear,
    Floating thro' an evening atmosphere,
Grow golden all about the sky ;
In thee, all passion becomes passionless,
Touch'd by thy spirit's mellowness,
Losing his fire and active might
    In a silent meditation,
Falling into a still delight,

And luxury of contemplation :
As waves that up a quiet cove
    Rolling slide, and lying still
    Shadow forth the banks at will:
Or sometimes they swell and move
    Pressing up against the land,
    With motions of the outer sea :
      And the self-same influence
      Controlleth all the soul and sense
Of Passion gazing upon thee,
His bow-string slacken'd, languid Love,
    Leaning his cheek upon his hand,
    Droops both his wings, regarding thee,
    And so would languish evermore,
    Serene, imperial Eleänore.

I watch thy grace ; and in its place
My heart a charm'd slumber keeps,
While I muse upon thy face.
  .   .   .   .

———

PALE was the perfect face . . . and meek
Seemed the full lips, and mild the luminous
    eyes.

MAUD.

She has neither savor nor salt
But a cold and clear-cut face.   .   .   .
Perfectly beautiful: let it be granted her:
    where is the fault ?
All that I saw (for her eyes were downcast, not
    to be seen)
Faultily faultless, icily regular, splendidly null,
Dead perfection, no more ; nothing more, if it
    had not been
For a chance of travel, a paleness, an hour's de-
    fect of the rose,
Or an underlip, you may call it a little too ripe,
    too full,
Or the least little delicate aquiline curve in a
    sensitive nose,

.   .   .   .

Cold and clear-cut face, why come you so cruelly
    meek,

.   .   .   .

Pale with the golden beam of an eyelash dead
    on the cheek,
Passionless, pale, cold face, star-sweet on a
    gloom profound ;

.   .   .   .

Maud with her exquisite face,
And wild voice pealing up to the sunny sky,
And feet like sunny gems on an English green,
Maud in the light of her youth and her grace.

.   .   .   .

Silence, beautiful voice !
Be still, for you only trouble the mind
With a joy in which I cannot rejoice,
A glory I shall not find.
Still ! I will hear you no more,
For your sweetness hardly leaves me a choice
But to move to the meadow and fall before
Her feet on the meadow grass, and adore,
Not her, who is neither courtly nor kind,
Not her, not her, but a voice.

.   .   .   .

I have play'd with her when a child ;
She remembers it now we meet.
Ah well, well, well, I may be beguiled
By some coquettish deceit.
Yet, if she were not a cheat,
If Maud were all that she seem'd,
And her smile had all that I dream'd,
Then the world were not so bitter
But a smile could make it sweet.

.   .   .   .

'Tis a morning pure and sweet,
And a dewy splendor falls
On the little flower that clings
To the turrets and the walls;
'Tis a morning pure and sweet,
And the light and shadow fleet;
She is walking in the meadow,
And the woodland echo rings;
In a moment we shall meet;
She is singing in the meadow,
And the rivulet at her feet
Ripples on in light and shadow
To the ballad that she sings.

Do I hear her sing as of old,
My bird with the shining head,
My own dove with the tender eye?

————

On her mouth
A doubtful smile dwelt like a clouded moon
In a still water.

————

MARIANA.

She, as her carol sadder grew
    From brow and bosom slowly down
Thro' rosy taper fingers drew

Her streaming curls of deepest brown
To left and right, and made appear,
    Still-lighted in a secret shrine,
    Her melancholy eyes divine,   ,
The home of woe without a tear,
        And " Ave Mary," was her moan,
          " Madonna, sad is night and morn ; "
        And " Ah," she sang, "to be all alone,
          To live forgotten, and love forlorn."

Till all the crimson changed, and past
    Into deep orange o'er the sea,
Low on her knees herself she cast,
    Before Our Lady murmur'd she;
Complaining, "Mother, give me grace
    To help me of my weary load."
    And on the liquid mirror glow'd
The clear perfection of her face.
        " Is this the form," she made her moan,
          " That won his praises night and morn ? "
        And, " Ah," she said, "but I wake alone,
          I sleep forgotten, I wake forlorn."

COME INTO THE GARDEN, MAUD.

I.

Come into the garden, Maud,
  For the black bat, night, has flown,
Come into the garden, Maud,
  I am here at the gate alone;
And the woodbine spices are wafted abroad,
  And the musk of the roses blown.

II.

For a breeze of morning moves,
  And the planet of Love is on high,
Beginning to faint in the light that she loves
  On a bed of daffodil sky,
To faint in the light of the sun that she loves,
  To faint in his light, and to die.

III.

All night have the roses heard
  The flute, violin, bassoon;
All night has the casement jessamine stirr'd
  To the dancers dancing in tune;
Till a silence fell with the waking bird,
  And a hush with the setting moon.

IV.

I said to the lily, " There is but one
  With whom she has heart to be gay.
When will the dancers leave her alone?
  She is weary of dance and play."
Now half to the setting moon are gone,
  And half to the rising day ;
Low on the sand and loud on the stone
  The last wheel echoes away.

V.

I said to the rose, " The brief night goes
  In babble and revel and wine,
O young lord-lover, what sighs are those,
  For one that will never be thine ?
But mine, but mine," so I sware to the rose,
   " For ever and ever, mine."

VI.

And the soul of the rose went into my blood,
  As the music clash'd in the hall ;
And long by the garden lake I stood,
  For I heard your rivulet fall
From the lake to the meadow and on to the wood,
  Our wood, that is dearer than all.

VII.

From the meadow your walks have left so sweet
 That whenever a March-wind sighs
He sets the jewel-print of your feet
 In violets blue as your eyes,
To the woody hollows in which we meet
 And the valleys of Paradise.

VIII.

The slender acacia would not shake
 One long milk-bloom on the tree;
The white lake-blossom fell into the lake,
 As the pimpernel dozed on the lea;
But the rose was awake all night for your
  sake,
 Knowing your promise to me;
The lilies and roses were all awake,
 They sigh'd for the dawn and thee.

IX.

Queen rose of the rosebud garden of girls,
 Come hither, the dances are done,
In gloss of satin and glimmer of pearls,
 Queen lily and rose in one;
Shine out, little head, sunning over with curls,
 To the flowers, and be their sun.

X.

There has fallen a splendid tear
　From the passion-flower at the gate.
She is coming, my dove, my dear;
　She is coming, my life, my fate;
The red rose cries, " She is near, she is near; "
　And the white rose weeps, " She is late; "
The larkspur listens, " I hear, I hear; "
　And the lily whispers, " I wait."

XI.

She is coming, my own, my sweet;
　Were it ever so airy a tread,
My heart would hear her and beat,
　Were it earth in an earthy bed;
My dust would hear her and beat,
　Had I lain for a century dead;
Would start and tremble under her feet,
　And blossom in purple and red.

———

MARGARET.

O sweet pale Margaret,
O rare pale Margaret,
What lit your eyes with tearful power,
Like moonlight on a falling shower?

Who lent you, love, your mortal dower
  Of pensive thought and aspect pale,
  Your melancholy sweet and frail
As perfume of the cuckoo-flower?
From the westward-winding flood,
From the evening-lighted wood,
  From all things outward you have won
A tearful grace, as tho' you stood
  Between the rainbow and the sun.
The very smile before you speak
That dimples your transparent cheek,
  Encircles all the heart, and feedeth
The senses with a still delight
    Of dainty sorrow without sound,
    Like the tender amber round,
  Which the moon about her spreadeth
Moving thro' a fleecy night.

You love, remaining peacefully,
  To hear the murmur of the strife,
  But enter not the toil of life.
Your spirit is the calmed sea,
  Laid by the tumult of the fight.
You are the evening star, alway
  Remaining betwixt dark and bright;
Lull'd echoes of laborious day

Come to you, gleams of mellow light
Float by you on the verge of night.

A fairy shield your Genius made
   And gave you on your natal day.
Your sorrow, only sorrow's shade,
   Keeps real sorrow far away.
You move not in such solitudes,
   You are not less divine,
But more human in your moods,
   Than your twin-sister Adeline.
Your hair is darker, and your eyes
   Touch'd with a somewhat darker hue
   And less aërially blue.
But ever trembling thro' the dew
Of dainty-woeful sympathies.

   O sweet pale Margaret,
   O rare pale Margaret,
Come down, come down, and hear me speak:
Tie up the ringlets on your cheek:
   The sun is just about to set.
The arching limes are tall and shady,
   And faint, rainy lights are seen,
    Moving in the leafy beech,
Rise from the feast of sorrow, lady,

Where all day long you sit between
  Joy and woe, and whisper each.
Or only look across the lawn,
  Look out below your bower-eaves,
Look down, and let your blue eyes dawn
  Upon me thro' the jasmine-leaves.

———

PETULANT she spoke, and at herself she laughed;
A rosebud set with little wilful thorns,
And sweet as English air could make her.

———

BIRDS IN THE HIGH HALL–GARDEN.

I.

BIRDS in the high Hall-garden
  When twilight was falling,
Maud, Maud, Maud, Maud,
  They were crying and calling.

II.

Where was Maud ? in our wood;
  And I, who else, was with her,
Gathering woodland lilies
  Myriads blow together.

III.

Birds in our wood sang
  Ringing thro' the valleys,
Maud is here, here, here,
  In among the lilies.

IV.

I kiss'd her slender hand,
  She took the kiss sedately;
Maud is not seventeen,
  But she is tall and stately.

V.

I to cry out on pride
  Who have won her favor!
O Maud were sure of Heaven
  If lowliness could save her.

VI.

I know the way she went
  Home with her maiden posy,
For her feet have touch'd the meadows
  And left the daisies rosy.

VII.

Birds in the high Hall-garden
  Were crying and calling to her,

Where is Maud, Maud, Maud?
One is come to woo her.

VIII.

Look, a horse at the door,
 And little King Charles is snarling,
Go back, my lord, across the moor,
 You are not her darling.

THE GARDENER'S DAUGHTER.

THIS morning is the morning of the day,
When I and Eustace from the city went
To see the Gardener's Daughter.

 · · · · · · · · · ·

      Juliet, she
So light of foot, so light of spirit — oh! she
To me myself, for some three careless moons,
The summer pilot of an empty heart
Unto the shores of nothing! Know you not
Such touches are but embassies of love,
To tamper with the-feelings, ere he found
Empire for life? but Eustace painted her,
And said to me, she sitting with us then,
"When will you paint like this?" and I re-
  plied,

(My words were half in earnest, half in jest)
" 'Tis not your work, but Love's, Love, unper-
    ceived,
A more ideal Artist he than all,
Came, drew your pencil from you, made those
    eyes,
Darker than darkest pansies, and that hair
More black than ashbuds in the front of March."
And Juliet answer'd laughing, "Go and see
The Gardener's daughter : trust me after that,
You scarce can fail to match his masterpiece."
And up we rose, and on the spur we went.

.   .   .   .

           Who has not heard
Of Rose, the Gardener's daughter ?

.   .   .   .

           Long before
I look'd upon her, when I heard her name
My heart was like a prophet to my heart,
And told me I should love. A crowd of hopes,
That sought to sow themselves like winged
    seeds,
Born out of everything I heard and saw,
Flutter'd about my senses and my soul:
And vague desires, like fitful blasts of balm
To one that travels quickly, made the air

Of Life delicious, and all kinds of thought
That verged upon them, sweeter than the dream
Dream'd by a happy man, when the dark East,
Unseen, is brightening to his bridal morn.   .
And sure this orbit of the memory folds
Forever in itself the day we went
To see her.

.   .   .   .

                    I turn'd
And, ere a star can wink, beheld her.   .   .   .
.   .   .   Up the porch there grew an Eastern rose,
That, flowering high, the last night's gale had
          caught,
And blown across the walk.   One arm aloft —
Gown'd in pure white, that fitted to the shape —
Holding the bush, to fix it back, she stood,
A single stream of all her soft brown hair
Pour'd on one side : the shadow of the flowers
Stole all the golden gloss, and, wavering
Lovingly lower, trembled on her waist —
Ah, happy shade — and still went wavering down,
But ere it touch'd a foot, that might have danced
The greensward into greener circles, dipt
And mix'd with shadows of the common ground !
But the full day dwelt on her brows, and sunn'd
Her violet eyes, and all her Hebe-bloom,

And doubled his own warmth against her lips,
And on the bounteous wave of such a breast
As never pencil drew.   Half light, half shade
She stood, a sight to make an old man young.
So rapt, we near'd the house ; but she, a Rose
In roses, mingled with her fragrant toil,
Nor heard us come, nor from her tendance turn'd
Into the world without ; till close at hand,
And almost ere I knew mine own intent,
This murmur broke the stillness of that air
Which brooded round about her :
                    " Ah, one rose,
One rose, but one by those fair fingers culled,
Were worth a hundred kisses press'd on lips
Less exquisite than thine ! "
                    She look'd : but all
Suffused with blushes — neither self-possess'd
Nor startled, but betwixt this mood and that,
Divided in a graceful quiet — paused,
And dropt the branch she held, and turning,
          wound
Her looser hair in braid, and stirr'd her lips
For some sweet answer, tho' no answer came ;
Nor yet refused the rose, but granted it,
And moved away, and left me, statue-like,
In act to render thanks.

I, that whole day,
Saw her no more, altho' I lingered there
Till every daisy slept, and Love's white star
Beamed through the thicken'd cedar in the dusk.

.　.　.　.　.　.　.　.　.　.

So home I went, but could not sleep for joy,
Reading her perfect features in the gloom,
Kissing the rose she gave me o'er and o'er,
And shaping faithful record of the glance
That graced the giving — such a noise of life
Swarm'd in the golden present, such a voice
Called to me from the years to come, and such
A length of bright horizon rimm'd the dark.
And all that night I heard the watchman peal
The sliding season: all that night I heard
The heavy clocks knolling the drowsy hours.
The drowsy hours, dispensers of all good,
O'er the mute city stole with folded wings,
Distilling odors on me as they went
To greet their fairer sisters of the East.
Love at first sight, first-born and heir to all,
Made this night thus. Henceforth squall nor
　　storm
Could keep me from that Eden where she dwelt.

.　.　.　.　.　.　.　.　.　.

.　.　. And more and more

A word could bring the color to my cheek;
A thought would fill my eyes with happy dew;
Love trebled life with me. . . . .

.   .   .   .

Day by day,
Like one that never can be wholly known,
Her beauty grew ; till Autumn brought an hour

.   .   .   .

Then   .   .   .   I spoke to her,
Requiring, tho' I knew it was mine own,
Yet for the pleasure that I took to hear,
Requiring at her hand the greatest gift,
.A woman's heart, the heart of her I loved ;
And in that time and place she answer'd me,
And in the compass of three little words,
More musical than ever came in one,
The silver fragments of a broken voice,
Made me most happy, faltering, "I am thine !"
    Shall I cease here ? Is this enough to say
That my desire, like all strongest hopes,
By its own energy fulfill'd itself,
Merged in completion ? Would you learn at
        full
How passion rose thro' circumstantial grades
Beyond all grades develop'd ? and indeed
I had not staid so long to tell you all,

But while I mused came Memory with sad eyes,
Holding the folded annals of my youth ;
And while I mused, Love with knit brows went
  by,
And with a flying finger swept my lips,
And spake, " Be wise : not easily forgiven
Are those, who setting wide the doors, that bar
The secret bridal chambers of the heart,
Let in the day." Here, then, my words have end.
 Yet might I tell of meetings, of farewells —
Of that which came between, more sweet than
  each,
In whispers, like the whispers of the leaves
That tremble round a nightingale — in sighs
Which perfect Joy, perplex'd for utterance,
Stole from her sister Sorrow. Might I not tell
Of difference, reconcilement, pledges given,
And vows, when there was never need of vows,
And kisses, where the heart on one wild leap
Hung tranced from all pulsation, as above
The heavens between their fairy fleeces pale
Sow'd all their mystic gulfs with fleeting stars;
Or while balmy glooming, crescent-lit,
Spread the light haze along the river-shores,
And in the hollows ; . . . .

. . . .

Behold her. . . . . . .
As I beheld her ere she knew my heart —
My first, last love; the idol of my youth,
The darling of my manhood, and, alas!
Now the most blessed memory of mine age.

DARLING KATIE.

A MAIDEN of our century, yet most meek;
A daughter of our meadows, yet not coarse;
Straight, but as lissome as a hazel wand;
Her eyes a bashful azure, and her hair .
In gloss and hue the chestnut, when the shell
Divides three-fold to show the fruit within.
.   .   .   .

Katie never ran; she moved
To meet me, winding under woodbine bowers
A little flutter'd, with her eyelids down,
Fresh apple-blossom, blushing for a boon.

All her thoughts as fair within her eyes,
As bottom agates seem to wave and float
In crystal currents of clear waving seas.

A HALF-DISDAIN
Perched on the proud blossom of her lips.

THE BEAUTY OF HOLINESS.

Behold her eyes
Beyond my knowing of them, beautiful,
Beyond all knowing of them, wonderful,
Beautiful in the light of holiness.

———

Mild deep eyes, upraised, that knew
    The beauty and repose of faith,
And the clear spirit shining thro'.

———

Her eyes are homes of silent prayer.

———

TRUE LOVE.

"He does not love me for my birth,
    Nor for my lands so broad and fair;
He loves me for my own true worth,
    And that is well," said Lady Clare.

———

And on her lover's arm she leant,
    And round her waist she felt it fold,
And far across the hills they went,
    In that new world which is the old.

ODE ON THE DEATH OF THE DUKE OF WELLINGTON.

I.

Bury the Great Duke
  With an empire's lamentation,

.   .   .   .

Lead out the pageant: sad and slow,
As fits an universal woe,

.   .   .   .

Mourn for the man of amplest influence,
Yet clearest of ambitious crime,
Our greatest yet with least pretense,
Great in council and great in war,
Foremost captain of his time,
Rich in saving common sense,
And, as the greatest only are,
In his simplicity sublime.
O good gray head which all men knew,
O voice from which their omens all men drew,
O iron nerve to true occasion true,
O fall'n at length that tower of strength
Which stood four-square to all the winds that
    blew !
Such was he whom we deplore.

.   .   .   .

II.

. . . . Remember all
He spoke among you, and the Man who spoke;
Who never sold the truth to serve the hour,
Nor palter'd with Eternal God for power;
Who let the turbid streams of rumor flow
Thro' either babbling world of high and low;
Whose life was work, whose language rife
With rugged maxims hewn from life;
Who never spoke against a foe.

. . . .

Let his great example stand
Colossal, seen of every land,
And keep the soldier firm, the statesman pure;

. . . .

Eternal honor to his name.

III.

Peace, it is a day of pain
For one about whose patriarchal knee
Late the little children clung:
O peace, it is a day of pain
For one, upon whose hand and heart and brain
Once the weight and fate of Europe hung.
Ours the pain, be his the gain!

More than is of man's degree
Must be with us, watching here
At this, our great solemnity.
Whom we see not we revere.

.   .   .   .

We revere, and while we hear
The tides of Music's golden sea
Setting toward eternity,
Uplifted high in heart and hope are we,
Until we doubt not that for one so true
There must be other nobler work to do.

.   .   .   .

For tho' the Giant Ages heave the hill
And break the shore, and evermore
Make and break, and work their will;
Tho' world on world in myriad myriads roll
Round us, each with different powers,
And other forms of life than ours,
What know we greater than the soul?
On God and Godlike men we build our trust.
Hush, the Dead March wails in the people's
    ears :
The dark crowd moves, and there are sobs and
    tears;
The black earth yawns : the mortal disappears;
Ashes to ashes, dust to dust;

He is gone who seem'd so great. —
Gone; but nothing can bereave him
Of the force he made his own
Being here, and we believe him
Something far advanced in state,
And that he wears a truer crown
Than any wreath that man can weave him.
Speak no more of his renown,
Lay your earthly fancies down,
And in the vast cathedral leave him.
God accept him, Christ receive him.

A HUSBAND'S TRIBUTE.

Look through mine eyes with thine, true wife,
　Round my true heart thine arms entwine :
My other dearer life in life,
　Look through my very soul with thine !
Untouched with any shade of years,
　May those kind eyes forever dwell !
They have not shed a many tears
　Dear eyes, since first I knew them well.

Yet tears they shed ; they had their part
　Of sorrow : for, when time was ripe,
The still affection of the heart
　Became an outward breathing type,

That into stillness past again,
　And left a want unknown before ;
Although the loss has brought us pain,
　That loss but made us love the more,

With farther lookings on.   The kiss,
　The woven arms, seem but to be
Weak symbols of the settled bliss,
　The comfort I have found in thee :
But that God bless thee, dear — who wrought
　Two spirits to one equal mind —
With blessings beyond hope or thought,
　With blessings which no words can find.

――――

MARRIED LOVERS.

Rose, on this terrace fifty years ago,
　When I was in my June, you in your May,
Two words, "My Rose," set all your face
　　aglow.
And now that I am white, and you are gray
That blush of fifty years ago, my dear,
　Blooms in the Past, but close to me to-day
As this red rose, which on our terrace here
　Glows in the blue of fifty miles away.

VICTORIA.

REVERED, beloved — O you that hold
 A nobler office upon earth
 Than arms, or power of brain or birth
Could give the warrior kings of old.

. . . .

 May children of our children say,
" She wrought her people lasting good;

" Her court was pure ; her life serene ;
 God gave her peace ; her land reposed ;
 A thousand claims to reverence closed
In her as Mother, Wife and Queen."

―――

LINES IN MEMORY OF THE LATE PRINCE CONSORT.

INDEED he seems to me
Scarce other than my own ideal knight,
Who reverenced his conscience as his king :
Whose glory was, redressing human wrong ;
Who spake no slander, no, nor listen'd to it;
Who loved one only, and who clave to her —
Her, over all whose realms, to their last isle,
Commingled with the gloom of imminent war,
The shadow of his love moved like eclipse

Darkening the world. We have lost him : he is
    gone :
We know him now ; all narrow jealousies
Are silent; and we see him as he moved,
How modest, kindly, all-accomplished, wise,
With what sublime repression of himself,
And in what limits, and how tenderly ;
Not swaying to this faction or to that ;
Not making his high place the lawless perch
Of wing'd ambitions, nor a vantage ground
For pleasure ; but thro' all this tract of years
Wearing the white flower of a blameless life,
Before a thousand peering littlenesses,
In that fierce light which beats upon a throne
And blackens every blot : for where is he
Who dares foreshadow for an only son
A lovelier life, a more unstained than his ?
Or how should England, dreaming of his sons
Hope more for these than some inheritance
Of such a life, a heart, a mind as thine,
Thou noble Father of her Kings to be ;
Laborious for her people and her poor,
Voice in the rich dawn of an ampler day,
Far-sighted summoner of war and waste
To fruitful strifes and rivalries of peace,
Sweet nature gilded by the gracious gleam

Of letters, dear to science, dear to art,
Dear to thy land and ours, a Prince indeed,
Beyond all titles, and a household name
Hereafter thro' all times, Albert the good.
Break not, O woman's heart, but still endure;
Break not, for thou art royal, but endure,
Remembering all the beauty of that star
Which shone so close beside ye, that ye made
One light together, but has past and left
The Crown a lonely splendor.　May all love,
His love, unseen, but felt, o'ershadow thee,
The love of all thy sons encompass thee,
The love of all thy daughters cherish thee,
The love of all thy people comfort thee,
Till God's love set thee at his side again.

THE PRINCESS.

ALL beauty compassed in a female form,
The Princess; liker to the inhabitant
Of some clear planet close upon the Sun,
Than our man's earth : Such eyes were in her
　　　　head,
And so much grace and power, breathing down
From over her arched brows, with every turn
Lived through her to the tips of her long hands,
And to her feet.　　　·

THE GRANDMOTHER.

I.

And Willy, my eldest-born, is gone, you say,
　　little Anne ?
Ruddy and white and strong on his legs, he
　　looks like a man.
And Willy's wife has written : she never was
　　over-wise,
Never the wife for Willy : he wouldn' take my
　　advice.

II.

For, Annie, you see, her father was not the man
　　to save,
Hadn't a head to manage, and drank himself
　　into his grave.
Pretty enough, very pretty ! but I was against
　　it for one.
Eh !— but he wouldn't hear me — and Willy,
　　you say, is gone.

III.

Willy, my beauty, my eldest-born, the flower of
　　the flock ;
Never a man could fling him : for Willy stood
　　like a rock.　　　·

" Here's a leg for a babe of a week!" says doc-
    tor: and he would be bound,
There was not his like that year in twenty
    parishes round.

IV.

Strong of his hands, and strong on his legs, but
    still of his tongue !
I ought to have gone before him : I wonder he
    went so young.
I cannot cry for him, Annie ; I have not long to
    stay ;
Perhaps I shall see him the sooner, for he lived
    far away.

V.

Why do you look at me, Annie ? you think I am
    hard and cold ;
But all my children have gone before me, I am
    so old :
I cannot weep for Willy, nor can I weep for the
    rest :
Only at your age, Annie, I could have wept with
    the best.

VI.

For I remember a quarrel I had with your
father, my dear,
All for a slanderous story, that cost me many a
tear.
I mean your grandfather, Annie; it cost me a
world of woe,
Seventy years ago, my darling, seventy years
ago.

VII.

For Jenny, my cousin, had come to the place,
and I knew right well
That Jenny had tript in her time: I knew, but
I would not tell.
And she to be coming and slandering me, the
base little liar!
But the tongue is a fire, as you know, my dear,
the tongue is a fire.

VIII.

And the parson made it his text that week, and
he said likewise,
That a lie which is half a truth is ever the
blackest of lies,

That a lie which is all a lie may be met and
    fought with outright,
But a lie which is part a truth is a harder mat-
    ter to fight.

IX.

And Willy had not been down to the farm for a
    week and a day ;
And all things look'd half dead, tho' it was the
    middle of May.
Jenny, to slander me, who knew what Jenny
    had been !
But soiling another, Annie, will never make
    one's self clean.

X.

And I cried myself well-nigh blind, and all of
    an evening late
I climb'd to the top of the garth, and stood by
    the road at the gate.
The moon like a rick on fire was rising over the
    dale,
And whit, whit, whit, in the bush beside me
    chirrupt the nightingale.

XI.

All of a sudden he stopt : then past by the gate
    of the farm,
Willy — he didn't see me — and Jenny hung
    on his arm.
Out into the road I started, and spoke I scarce
    knew how ;
Ah there's no fool like the old one — it makes
    me angry now.

XII.

Willy stood up like a man, and look'd the thing
    that he meant ;
Jenny, the viper, made me a mocking courtesy
    and went.
And I said, " Let us part : in a hundred years
    it'll be all the same,
You cannot love me at all, if you love not my
    good name."

XIII.

And he turn'd, and I saw his eyes all wet, in the
    sweet moonshine :
" Sweetheart, I love you so well that your good
    name is mine.

And what do I care for Jane, let her speak of
    you well or ill;
But marry me out of hand: we too shall be
    happy still!"

XIV.

"Marry you, Willy!" said I, "but I needs
    must speak my mind,
And I fear you'll listen to tales, be jealous and
    hard and unkind."
But he turn'd and claspt me in his arms, and
    answer'd, "No, love, no;"
Seventy years ago, my darling, seventy years ago.

XV.

So Willy and I were wedded: I wore a lilac
    gown;
And the ringers rang with a will, and he gave
    the ringers a crown.
But the first that ever I bare was dead before he
    was born,
Shadow and shine is life, little Annie, flower
    and thorn.

XVI.

That was the first time, too, that ever I thought
of death.
There lay the sweet little body that never had
drawn a breath.
I had not wept, little Annie, not since I had
been a wife:
But I wept like a child that day, for the babe
had fought for his life.

XVII.

His dear little face was troubled, as if with
anger or pain;
I look'd at the still little body — his trouble
had all been in vain.
For Willy I cannot weep, I shall see him another morn:
But I wept like a child for the child that was
dead before he was born.

XVIII.

But he cheer'd me, my good man, for he seldom
said me nay:
Kind, like a man, was he; like a man, too, would
have his way:

Never jealous — not he : we had many a happy
    year ;
And he died, and I could not weep — my own
    time seem'd so near.

XIX.

But I wish'd it had been God's will that I, too,
    then could have died :
I began to be tired a little, and fain had slept at
    his side.
And that was ten years back, or more, if I don't
    forget:
But as to the children, Annie, they're all about
    me yet.

XX.

Pattering over the boards, my Annie who left
    me at two,
Patter she goes, my own little Annie, an Annie
    like you :
Pattering over the boards, she comes and goes at
    her will,
While Harry is in the five-acre and Charlie
    ploughing the hill.

XXI.

And Harry and Charlie, I hear them too — they
    sing to their team;
Often they come to the door in a pleasant kind
    of dream.
They come and sit by my chair, they hover
    about my bed —
I am not always certain if they be alive or dead.

XXII.

And yet I know for a truth, there's none of them
    left alive;
For Harry went at sixty, your father at sixty-
    five:
And Willy, my eldest-born, at nigh threescore
    and ten;
I knew them all as babies, and now they're
    elderly men.

XXIII.

For mine is a time of peace, it is not often I
    grieve;
I am oftener sitting at home in my father's farm
    at eve:

And the neighbors come and laugh and gossip,
    and so do I ;
I find myself often laughing at things that have
    long gone by.

XXIV.

To be sure the preacher says, our sins should
    make us sad :
But mine is a time of peace, and there is Grace
    to be had ;
And God, not man, is the Judge of us all when
    life shall cease ;
And in this Book, little Annie, the message is
    one of Peace.

XXV.

And age is a time of peace, so it be free from
    pain,
And happy has been my life; but I would not
    live it again.
I seem to be tired a little, that's all, and long for
    rest :
Only at your age, Annie, I could have wept with
    the best.

XXVI.

So Willy has gone, my beauty, my eldest-born,
    my flower;
But how can I weep for Willy, he has but gone
    for an hour —
Gone for a minute, my son, from this room into
    the next;
I, too, shall go in a minute. What time have I
    to be vext ?

XXVII.

And Willy's wife has written, she never was
    over-wise.
Get me my glasses, Annie : thank God that I
    keep my eyes.
There is but a trifle left you, when I shall have
    past away,
But stay with the old woman now ; you cannot
    have long to stay.

———

MAIDENHOOD.

SEVENTEEN — and knew eight languages — in
    music
Peerless — her needle perfect, and her learning

Beyond the churchman: yet so meek, so
    modest,
So wife-like humble. . . . .

 .   .   .   .

Seventeen — a rose of grace !
Girl never breathed to rival such a rose :
Rose never blew that equall'd such a bud.

THE BEGGAR MAID.

HER arms across her breast she laid;
    She was more fair than words can say :
Barefooted came the beggar maid
    Before the king Cophetua.
In robe and crown the king stept down,
    To meet and greet her on her way;
"It is no wonder," said the lords,
    "She is more beautiful than day."

As shines the moon in clouded skies,
    She in her poor attire was seen :
One praised her ankles, one her eyes,
    One her dark hair and lovesome mien.
So sweet a face, such angel grace,
    In all that land had never been :

Cophetua sware a royal oath :
"This beggar-maid shall be my queen!"

―――

MEN are God's trees, and women are God's flowers.

―――

THE MAY QUEEN.

YOU must wake and call me early, call me early,
    mother dear;
To-morrow 'ill be the happiest time of all the
    glad New-year;
Of all the glad New-year, mother, the maddest
    merriest day;
For I'm to be Queen o' the May, mother, I'm to
    be Queen o' the May.

There's many a black, black eye, they say, but
    none so bright as mine;
There's Margaret and Mary, there's Kate and
    Caroline:
But none so fair as little Alice in all the land
    they say,
So I'm to be Queen o' the May, mother, I'm to
    be Queen o' the May.

I sleep so sound all night, mother, that I shall
    never wake,
If you do not call me loud when the day begins
    to break :
But I must gather knots of flowers, and buds
    and garland gay,
For I'm to be Queen o' the May, mother, I'm to
    be Queen o' the May.

As I came up the valley whom think ye should
    I see,
But Robin leaning on the bridge beneath the
    hazel-tree ?
He thought of that sharp look, mother, I gave
    him yesterday —
But I'm to be Queen o' the May, mother, I'm to
    be Queen o' the May.

He thought I was a ghost, mother, for I was all
    in white,
And I ran by him without speaking, like a flash
    of light.
They call me cruel-hearted, but I care not what
    they say,
For I'm to be Queen o' the May, mother, I'm to
    be Queen o' the May.

They say he's dying all for love, but that can
    never be :
They say his heart is breaking, mother — what is
    that to me ?
There's many a bolder lad 'ill woo me any sum-
    mer day,
And I'm to be Queen o' the May, mother, I'm to
    be Queen o' the May.

Little Effie shall go with me to-morrow to the
    green,
And you'll be there, too, mother, to see me made
    the Queen ;
For the shepherd lads on every side 'ill come from
    far away,
And I'm to be Queen o' the May, mother, I'm to
    be Queen o' the May.

The honeysuckle round the porch has wov'n its
    wavy bowers,
And by the meadow-trenches blow the faint
    sweet cuckoo-flowers ;
And the wild marsh-marigold shines like fire in
    swamps and hollows gray,
And I'm to be Queen o' the May, mother, I'm to
    be Queen o' the May.

The night-winds come and go, mother, upon the
    meadow-grass,
And the happy stars above them seem to brighten
    as they pass;
There will not be a drop of rain the whole of the
    livelong day,
And I'm to be Queen o' the May, mother, I'm to
    be Queen o' the May.

All the valley, mother, 'ill be fresh and green
    and still,
And the cowslip and the crowfoot are over all
    the hill,
And the rivulet in the flowery dale, 'ill merrily
    glance and play,
For I'm to be Queen o' the May, mother, I'm to
    be Queen o' the May.

So you must wake and call me early, call me
    early, mother dear,
To-morrow 'ill be the happiest time of all the
    glad New-year :
To-morrow 'ill be of all the year the maddest
    merriest day,
For I'm to be Queen o' the May, mother, I'm to
    be Queen o' the May.

NEW–YEAR'S EVE.

If you're waking call me early, call me early,
    mother dear,
For I would see the sun rise upon the glad New-
    year.
It is the last New-year that I shall ever see,
Then you may lay me low i' the mould and think
    no more of me.

To-night I saw the sun set: he set and left
    behind
The good old year, the dear old time, and all my
    peace of mind;
And the New-year's coming up, mother, but I
    shall never see
The blossom on the blackthorn, the leaf upon
    the tree.

Last May we made a crown of flowers: we had
    a merry day,
Beneath the hawthorn on the green they made
    me Queen of May;
And we danced about the May-pole and in the
    hazel copse,
Till Charles's Wain came out above the tall
    white chimney-tops.

There's not a flower on all the hills ; the frost
    is on the pane :
I only wish to live till the snowdrops come
    again :
I wish the snow would melt and the sun come
    out on high :
I long to see a flower so before the day I die.

The building rook 'ill caw from the windy tall
    elm-tree,
And the tufted plover pipe along the fallow
    lea,
And the swallow 'ill come back again with sum-
    mer o'er the wave,
But I shall lie alone, mother, within the mould-
    ering grave.

Upon the chancel-casement, and upon that grave
    of mine,
In the early early morning the summer sun 'ill
    shine,
Before the red cock crows from the farm upon
    the hill,
When you are warm-asleep, mother, and all the
    world is still.

When the flowers come again, mother, beneath
    the waning light
You'll never see me more in the long gray fields
    at night ;
When from the dry dark wold the summer airs
    blow cool
On the oat-grass and the sword-grass, and the
    bulrush in the pool.

You'll bury me, my mother, just beneath the
    hawthorn shade,
And you'll come sometimes and see me when I
    am lowly laid,
I shall not forget you, mother, I shall hear you
    when you pass,
With your feet above my head in the long and
    pleasant grass.

I have been wild and wayward, but you'll for-
    give me now ;
You'll kiss me, my own mother, upon my cheek
    and brow ;
Nay, nay, you must not weep, nor let your grief
    be wild,
You should not fret for me, mother, you have
    another child.

If I can I'll come again, mother, from out my
    resting-place;
Tho' you'll not see me, mother, I shall look upon
    your face;
Tho' I cannot speak a word, I shall hearken
    what you say,
And be often, often with you when you think
    I'm far away.

Good-night, good-night, when I have said good-
    night for evermore,
And you see me carried out from the threshold of
    the door;
Don't let Effie come to see me till my grave be
    growing green;
She'll be a better child to you than ever I have
    been.

She'll find my garden-tools upon the granary
    floor;
Let her take 'em; they are hers: I shall never
    garden more:
But tell her, when I'm gone, to train the rose-
    bush that I set
About the parlor-window and the box of mignon-
    ette.

Good-night, sweet mother; call me before the
    day is born,
All night I lie awake, but I fall asleep at morn;
But I would see the sun rise upon the glad New-
    year,
So, if you're waking, call me, call me early,
    mother dear.

CONCLUSION.

I THOUGHT to pass away before, and yet alive I am;
And in the fields all round I hear the bleating
    of the lamb.
How sadly, I remember, rose the morning of the
    year!
To die before the snowdrop came, and now the
    violet's here.

O sweet is the new violet, that comes beneath
    the skies,
And sweeter is the young lamb's voice to me
    that cannot rise,
And sweet is all the land about, and all the
    flowers that blow,
And sweeter far is death than life to me that
    long to go.

It seem'd so hard at first, mother, to leave the
  blessed sun,
And now it seems as hard to stay, and yet, His
  will be done!
But still I think it can't be long before I find
  release;
And that good man, the clergyman, has told me
  words of peace.

O blessings on his kindly voice and on his
  silver hair!
And blessings on his whole life long, until he
  meet me there!
O blessings on his kindly heart and on his
  silver head!
A thousand times I blest him, as he knelt beside my bed.

He taught me all the mercy, for he show'd me
  all the sin.
Now, tho' my lamp was lighted late, there's
  One will let me in:
Nor would I now be well, mother, again, if that
  could be,
For my desire is but to pass to Him that died
  for me.

I did not hear the dog howl, mother, or the
    death-watch beat,
There came a sweeter token when the night and
    morning meet:
But sit beside my bed, mother, and put your
    hand in mine,
And Effie on the other side, and I will tell the
    sign.

All in the wild March-morning I heard the
    angels call;
It was when the moon was setting, and the dark
    was over all;
The trees began to whisper, and the wind be-
    gan to roll,
And in the wild March-morning I heard them
    call my soul.

For lying broad awake, I thought of you and
    Effie dear;
I saw you sitting in the house, and I no longer
    here;
With all my strength I pray'd for both, and so
    I felt resign'd,
And up the valley came a swell of music on the
    wind.

I thought that it was fancy, and I listen'd in
    my bed,
And then did something speak to me — I know
    not what was said;
For great delight and shuddering took hold of
    all my mind,
And up the valley came again the music on the
    wind.

But you were sleeping : and I said, " It's not for
    them ; it's mine."
And if it comes three times, I thought, I take it
    for a sign.
And once again it came, and close beside the
    window-bars,
Then seem'd to go right up to Heaven and die
    among the stars.

So now I think my time is near. I trust it is.
    I know
The blessed music went that way my soul will
    have to go.
And for myself, indeed, I care not if I go to-
    day.
But, Effie, you must comfort her when I am
    past away.

And say to Robin a kind word, and tell him not
    to fret ;
There's many worthier than I, would make him
    happy yet.
If I had lived — I cannot tell — I might have
    been his wife;
But all these things have ceased to be, with my
    desire of life.

O look! the sun begins to rise, the heavens are
    in a glow ;
He shines upon a hundred fields, and all of them
    I know,
And there I move no longer now, and there his
    light may shine —
Wild flowers in the valley for other hands than
    mine.

O sweet and strange it seems to me, that ere
    this day is done
The voice, that now is speaking, may be beyond
    the sun —
Forever and forever with those just souls and
    true —
And what is life, that we should moan ? why
    make we such ado ?

Forever and forever, all in a blessed home —
And there to wait a little while till you and
      Effie come —
To lie within the light of God, as I lie upon
      your breast —
And the wicked cease from troubling, and the
      weary are at rest.

Part Third.

IMMORTELLES.

CROSSING THE BAR.

Sunset and evening star,
  And one clear call for me ;
And may there be no moaning of the bar
  When I put out to sea.

But such a tide as moving seems asleep,
  Too full for sound and foam
When that which drew from out the boundless
      deep
  Turns again home.

Twilight and evening bell,
  And after that the dark !
And may there be no sadness of farewell,
  When I embark ;

For tho' from out the bourne of Time and Place
  The flood may bear me far,
I hope to see my Pilot face to face
  When I have crost the bar.

———

One Heaven receives us all,
How sweet to have a common faith
To hold a common scorn of death !

IMMORTAL LOVE.

Strong Son of God immortal Love,
 Whom we, that have not seen thy face
 By faith, and faith alone embrace,
Believing where we cannot prove;

Thine are these orbs of light and shade —
 Thou madest Life in man and brute;
 Thou madest Death: and lo! thy foot
Is on the skull which thou hast made.

Thou wilt not leave us in the dust:
 Thou madest man, he knows not why;
 He thinks he was not made to die;
And thou hast made him: thou art just.

Thou seemest human and divine,
 The highest, holiest manhood, thou:
 Our wills are ours, we know not how;
Our wills are ours, to make them thine.

Our little systems have their day;
 They have their day and cease to be;
 They are but broken lights of thee,
And thou, O Lord, art more than they.

We have but faith: we cannot know;
 For knowledge is of things we see;
 And yet we trust it comes from thee,
A beam in darkness: let it grow.

Let knowledge grow from more to more,
 But more of reverence in us dwell:
 That mind and soul, according well,
May make one music, as before.

But vaster. We are fools and slight;
 We mock thee when we do not fear:
 But help thy foolish ones to bear;
Help thy vain worlds to bear thy light.

. . . .

Forgive my grief for one removed,
 Thy creature, whom I found so fair.
 I trust he lives in thee, and there
I find him worthier to be loved.

BE NEAR ME.

Be near me when my light is low,
 When the blood creeps, and the nerves prick
 And tingle; and the heart is sick,
And all the wheels of Being slow.

Be near me when the sensuous frame
   Is racked with pangs that conquer trust,
   And Time, a maniac, scattering dust,
And Life, a Fury, slinging flame.

Be near me when my faith is dry,
   And men the flies of latter spring,
   That lay their eggs, and sting and sing,
And weave their petty cells and die.

Be near me when I fade away,
   To point the term of human strife,
   And on the low, dark verge of life,
The twilight of eternal day.

Do we indeed desire the dead
   Should still be near us at our side?
   Is there no baseness we would hide?
No inner vileness that we dread?

Shall he for whose applause I strove,
   I had such reverence for his blame,
   See with clear eye some hidden shame,
And I be lessen'd in his love?

I wrong the grave with fears untrue :
    Shall love be blamed for want of faith ?
    There must be wisdom with great Death ;
The dead shall look me through and through.

Be near us when we climb or fall ;
    Ye watch, like God, the rolling hours
    With larger, other eyes than ours,
To make allowance for us all.

TRUST.

O, YET we trust that somehow good
    Will be the final goal of ill,
    To pangs of nature, sins of will,
Defects of doubt, and taints of blood ;

That nothing walks with aimless feet ;
    That not one life shall be destroyed,
    Or cast as rubbish to the void,
When God hath made the pile complete ;

That not a worm is cloven in vain ;
    That not a moth with vain desire
    Is shriveled in a fruitless fire,
Or but subserves another's gain.

Behold ! we knew not anything ;
 I can but trust that good shall fall
 At last — far off — at last, to all,
And every winter change to spring.

So runs my dream : but what am I ?
 An infant crying in the night ;
 An infant crying for the light ;
And with no language but a cry.

ST. AGNES.

DEEP on the convent-roof the snows
 Are sparkling to the moon :
My breath to Heaven like vapor goes ;
 May my soul follow soon !
The shadow of the convent-towers
 Slant down the snowy sward,
Still creeping with the creeping hours
 That lead me to my Lord :
Make Thou my spirit pure and clear
 As are the frosty skies,
Or this first snowdrop of the year
 That in my bosom lies.

As these white robes are soil'd and dark,
 To yonder shining ground ;

As this pale taper's earthly spark,
  To yonder argent round;
So shows my soul before the Lamb,
  My spirit before Thee:
So in mine earthly house I am,
  To that I hope to be.
Break up the heavens, O Lord! and far,
  Through all yon starlight keen,
Draw me, thy bride, a glittering star,
  In raiment white and clean.

He lifts me to the golden doors;
  The flashes come and go;
All Heaven bursts her starry floors,
  And strews her lights below,
And deepens on and up! the gates
  Roll back, and far within
For me the Heavenly Bridegroom waits,
  To make me pure of sin.
The Sabbaths of Eternity,
  One Sabbath deep and wide —
A light upon the shining sea —
  The Bridegroom with his bride.

TO A FRIEND IN SORROW.

THE wind, that beats the mountain, blows
    More softly round the open wold,
And gently comes the world to those
    That are cast in gentle mould.

And me this knowledge bolder made,
    Or else I had not dared to flow
In these words toward you, and invade
    Even with a verse your holy woe.

'Tis strange that those we lean on most,
    Those in whose laps our limbs are nursed,
Fall into shadow, soonest lost,
    Those we love first are taken first.

God gives us love.   Something to love
    He lends us; but, when love is grown
To ripeness, that on which it throve
    Falls off, and love is left alone.

.   .   .   .

I have not looked upon you nigh,
    Since that dear soul hath fallen asleep.
Great Nature is more wise than I:
    I will not tell you not to weep.

And though my own eyes fill with dew,
   Drawn from the spirit through the brain,
I will not even preach to you,
   Weep, weeping dulls the inward pain.

Let Grief be her own mistress still.
   She loveth her own anguish deep
More than much pleasure — Let her will
   Be done — to weep or not to weep.

I will not say " God's ordinance
   Of Death is blown in every wind,"
For that is not a common chance
   That takes away a noble mind.

.   .   .   .

Words weaker than your grief would make
   Grief more.

.   .   .   .

Sleep sweetly, tender heart, in peace :
   Sleep, holy spirit, blessed soul,
While the stars burn, the moons increase,
   And the great ages onward roll.

Sleep till the end, true soul and sweet,
   Nothing comes to thee new or strange;
Sleep full of rest from head to feet :
   Lie still, dry dust, secure of change.

HONEST DOUBT.

You say, but with no touch of scorn,
  Sweet-hearted you, whose light-blue eyes
  Are tender over drowning flies,
You tell me, doubt is Devil-born.

I know not: one indeed I knew
  In many subtle questions versed,
  Who touched a jarring lyre at first,
But ever strove to make it true :

Perplexed in faith, but pure in deeds,
  At last he beat his music out.
  There lives more faith in honest doubt,
Believe me, than in half the creeds.

He fought his doubts and gathered strength,
  He would not make his judgment blind,
  He faced the specters of the mind
And laid them: thus he came at length

To find a stronger faith his own ;
  And Power was with him in the night,
  Which makes the darkness and the light,
And dwells not in the light alone,

But in the darkness and the cloud,
  As over Sinai's peaks of old,
  While Israel made their gods of gold,
Although the tempest blew so loud.

_____

KNOWN AND UNKNOWN.

Dear friend, far off, my lost desire,
  So far, so near, in woe and weal;
  O, loved the most, when most I feel
There is a lower and a higher.

Known and unknown, human, divine!
  Sweet human hand and lips and eye;
  Dear heavenly friend that canst not die,
Mine, mine, forever, ever mine!

Strange friend, past, present, and to be;
  Loved deeplier, darklier understood;
  Behold, I dream a dream of good,
And mingle all the world with thee.

Thy voice is on the rolling air;
  I hear thee where the waters run;
  Thou standest in the rising sun,
And in the setting thou art fair.

Far off thou art, but ever nigh ;
   I have thee still, and I rejoice ;
   I prosper, circled with thy voice ;
I shall not lose thee tho' I die.

COMMUNION.

How pure at heart and sound in head,
   With what divine affections bold,
   Should be the man whose thoughts would hold
An hour's communion with the dead.

In vain shalt thou, or any, call
   The spirits from their golden day,
   Except, like them, thou too canst say,
My spirit is at peace with all.

BEYOND.

WE ranging down this lower track,
   The path we came by, thorn and flower,
   Is shadowed by the growing hour,
Lest life should fail in looking back.

So be it : there no shade can last
   In that deep dawn behind the tomb,
   But clear from marge to marge shall bloom
The eternal landscape of the past :

A lifelong tract of time revealed ;
　The fruitful hours of still increase ;
　Days ordered in a wealthy peace,
And those five years its richest field.

O Love ! thy province were not large,
　A bounded field, nor stretching far,
　Look also, Love, a brooding star,
A rosy warmth from marge to marge.

———

PAST AND PRESENT.

AND was the day of my delight
　As pure and perfect as I say ?
　The very source and fount of Day
Is dashed with wandering isles of night.

If all was good and fair we met,
　This earth had been the Paradise
　It never looked to human eyes
Since Adam left his garden yet.

And is it that the haze of grief
　Hath stretched my former joy so great?
　The lowness of the present state
That sets the past in this relief ?

Or that the past will always win
  A glory from its being far ;
  And orb into the perfect star
We saw not, when we moved therein?

  Nor blame I Death, because he bear
  The use of virtue out of Earth ;
  I know transplanted human worth
  Will bloom to profit, other where.

Thrice blest whose lives are faithful prayers,
Whose loves in higher love endure.

THE WISH.

  The wish that of the living whole
    No life may fail beyond the grave —
    Derives it not from what we have
  The likest God within the soul ?

  Are God and Nature then at strife,
    That Nature lends such evil dreams ?
    So careful of the type she seems,
  So careless of the single life ;

That I, considering everywhere
   Her secret meaning in her deeds,
   And finding that of fifty seeds
She often brings but one to bear,

I falter where I firmly trod,
   And falling with my weight of cares
   Upon the great world's altar-stairs,
That slope through darkness up to God,

I stretch lame hands of faith, and grope,
   And gather dust and chaff, and call
   To what I feel is Lord of all,
And faintly trust the larger hope.

BETTER TO LOVE.

I ENVY not, in any moods,
   The captive void of noble rage,
   The linnet born within the cage
That never knew the summer woods;

I envy not the beast that takes
   His license in the field of time,
   Unfettered by the sense of crime,
To whom a conscience never wakes;

Nor, what may count itself as blest,
  The heart that never plighted troth,
  But stagnates in the weeds of sloth,
Nor any want-begotten rest.

I hold it true what 'er befall;
  I feel it when I sorrow most;
  'Tis better to have loved and lost
Than never to have loved at all.

"BREAK, BREAK, BREAK."

BREAK, break, break,
  On thy cold gray stones, O Sea!
And I would that my tongue could utter
  The thoughts that arise in me.

O well for the fisherman's boy
  That he shouts with his sister at play!
O well for the sailor lad
  That he sings in his boat on the bay!

And the stately ships go on
  To the haven under the hill;
But oh! for the touch of a vanished hand,
  And the sound of a voice that is still!

Break, break, break,
 At the foot of thy crags, O Sea!
But the tender grace of a day that is dead,
 Will never come back to me.

IN LIGHT.

THAT each, who seems a separate whole,
 Should move his rounds, and fusing all
 The skirts of self again, should fall
Remerging in the general Soul.

Is faith as vague as all unsweet:
 Eternal form shall still divide
 The eternal soul from all beside;
And I shall know him when we meet:

And we shall sit at endless feast,
 Enjoying each the other's good:
 What vaster dream can hit the mood
Of Love on earth? He seeks at least

Upon the last and sharpest height,
 Before the spirits fade away,
 Some landing-place to clasp and say,
" Farewell! We lose ourselves in light."

FAREWELL.

THE slow sweet hours that bring us all things
    good,
The slow sad hours that bring us all things ill,
And all good things from evil, brought the
    night
In which we sat together and alone,
And to the want, that hollowed all the heart,
Gave utterance by the yearning of an eye,
That burned upon its object through such tears
As glow but once a life.

.   .   .   .

Farewell, like endless welcome, lived and died.
Then followed counsel, comfort, and the words
That make a man feel strong in speaking truth;
Till now the dark was worn, and overhead
The lights of sunset and of sunrise mixed
In that brief night: the summer night, that
    paused
Among her stars to hear us; stars that hung
Love-charmed to listen; all the wheels of Time
Spun round in station, but the end had come.
O then like those, who clench their nerves to
    rush
Upon their dissolution, we two rose,

There — closing like an individual life —
In one blind cry of passion and of pain,
Like bitter accusation even to death,
Caught up the whole of love and utter'd it,
And bade adieu for ever.
     Live — yet live —
Shall sharpest pathos blight us, knowing all
Life needs for life is possible to will —
Live happy; tend thy flowers; be tended by
My blessing! Should my shadow cross thy
   thoughts
Too sadly for their peace, remand it thou
For calmer hours to Memory's darkest hold,
If not to be forgotten — not at once —
Not all forgotten. Should it cross thy dreams,
O might it come like one that looks content,
With quiet eyes unfaithful to the truth,
And point thee forward to a distant light,
Or seem to lift a burthen from thy heart
And leave thee freer, till thou wake refresh'd,
Then when the low matin-chirp hath grown
Full choir, and morning driv'n her plough of
   pearl
Far furrowing into light the mounded rack,
Beyond the fair green field and eastern sea.

TEARS.

Tears . . .

.   .   .   .

Which weep a loss forever new,
  A void where heart on heart reposed;
  And, where warm hands have pressed and
     closed,
Silence, till I be silent too.

Which weep the comrade of my choice,
  An awful thought, a life removed,
  The human-hearted man I loved,
A Spirit, not a breathing voice.

Come, Time, and teach me many years
  I do not suffer in a dream;
  For now so strange do these things seem,
Mine eyes have leisure for their tears.

——

UNREST.

To-night the winds begin to rise
  And roar from yonder dropping day;
  The last red leaf is whirl'd away,
The rooks are blown about the skies;

The forest crack'd, the waters curl'd,
  The cattle huddled on the lea ;
  And wildly dashed on tower and tree
The sunbeam strikes along the world :

And but for fancies, which aver
  That all thy motions gently pass
  Athwart a plane of molten glass,
I scarce could brook the strain and stir

That makes the barren branches loud ;
  And but for fear it is not so,
  The wild unrest that lives in woe
Would dote and pore on yonder cloud

That rises upward always higher,
  And onward drags a laboring breast,
  And topples round the dreary west,
A looming bastion fringed with fire.

THE NATIVE LAND.

'Tis well, 'tis something, we may stand
  Where he in English earth is laid,
  And from his ashes may be made
The violet of his native land.

'Tis little; but it looks in truth
 As if the quiet bones were blest
 Among familiar names to rest
And in the places of his youth.

Come then, pure hands, and bear the head
 That sleeps; or wears the mask of sleep,
 And come, whatever loves to weep,
And hear the ritual of the dead.

Ah! yet, even yet, if this might be,
 I, falling on his faithful heart,
 Would, breathing through his lips, impart
The life that almost dies in me;

That dies not, but endures with pain,
 And slowly forms the firmer mind,
 Treasuring the look it cannot find,
The words that are not heard again.

LESSER GRIEFS.

THE lesser griefs, that may be said,
 That breathe a thousand tender vows,
 Are but as servants in a house
Where lies the master newly dead;

Who speak their feeling as it is,
    And weep the fulness from the mind :
    "It will be hard," they say, "to find
Another service such as this."

My lighter moods are like to these,
    That out of words a comfort win;
    But there are other griefs within,
And tears that at their fountain freeze:

For by the hearth the children sit
    Cold in that atmosphere of Death,
    And scarce endure to draw the breath,
Or like to noiseless phantoms flit:

But open converse is there none,
    So much the vital spirits sink
    To see the vacant chair, and think,
"How good ! How kind ! and he is gone."

THE SHADOW.

Now, sometimes in my sorrow shut,
    Or breaking into song by fits,
    Alone, alone, to where he sits,
The Shadow cloak'd from head to foot,

Who keeps the keys of all the creeds,
   I wander, often falling lame,
   And looking back from whence I came,
Or on to where the pathway leads;

And crying, " How changed from where it ran
   Thro' lands where not a leaf was dumb ;
   But all the lavish hills would hum
The murmur of a happy Pan :

" When each by turns was guide to each,
   And Fancy light from Fancy caught,
   And Thought leapt out to wed with Thought
Ere Thought could wed itself with Speech;

" And all we met was fair and good,
   And all was good that Time could bring,
   And all the secret of the Spring
Moved in the chambers of the blood;

" And many an old philosophy
   On Argive heights divinely sang,
   And round us all the thicket rang
To many a flute of Arcady."

MIGHTY LOVE.

I know that this was Life — the track
  Whereon with equal feet we fared:
  And then, as now, the day prepared
The daily burden for the back.

But this it was that made me move
  As light as carrier-birds in air;
  I loved the weight I had to bear,
Because it needed help of Love;

Nor could I weary, heart or limb,
  When mighty Love would cleave in twain
  The lading of a single pain,
And part it, giving half to him.

SORROW.

O sorrow, cruel fellowship!
  O Priestess in the vaults of Death!
  O sweet and bitter in a breath,
What whispers from thy lying lip?

"The stars," she whispers, "blindly run:
  A web is woven across the sky;
  From out waste places comes a cry,
And murmurs from the dying sun:

" And all the phantom, Nature, stands —
　　With all her music in her tone,
　　A hollow echo of my own —
A hollow form with empty hands."

And shall I take a thing so blind,
　　Embrace her as my natural good ;
　　Or crush her, like a vice of blood,
Upon the threshold of the mind ?

————

ENDURING BEAUTY.

THIS wall of solid flesh that comes between
　　　your soul and mine,
　　Will vanish and give place to the beauty that
　　　endures.

The beauty that endures on the Spiritual height,
　　When we shall stand transfigured, like Christ
　　　on Hermon hill,
And moving each to music, soul in soul and
　　　light in light,
　　Shall flash thro' one another in a moment as
　　　we will.

GAIN BY LOSS.

Though much is taken, much abides; and
    though
We are not now that strength which in old days
Moved earth and heaven: that which we are,
    we are :

.   .   .   .

Made weak by time and fate, but strong in will
To strive, to seek, to find, and not to yield.

THE DESERTED HOUSE.

Life and Thought have gone away
    Side by side,
    Leaving door and windows wide ;
Careless tenants they !

All within is dark as night :
In the windows.is no light :
And no murmur at the door,
So frequent on its hinge before.

Close the door, the shutters close,
    Or thro' the windows we shall see
    The nakedness and vacancy
Of the dark deserted house.

Come away : no more of mirth
    Is here or merry-making sound.
The house was builded of the earth,
    And shall fall again to ground.

Come away : for Life and Thought
    Here no longer dwell :
      But in a city glorious —
A great and distant city — have bought
    A mansion incorruptible.
      Would they could have staid with us !

THE SEASONS.

WE sleep and wake and sleep, but all things move :
The Sun flies forward to his brother Sun ;
The dark Earth follows wheeled in her ellipse :
And human things returning on themselves
Move onward, leading up the golden year.
"Ah! though the times, when some new thought
      can bud,
Are but as poet's seasons when they flower,
Yet seas, that daily gain upon the shore,
Have ebb and flow conditioning their march,
And slow and sure comes up the golden year.
When wealth no more shall rest in mounded
      heaps,

But smit with freer light shall slowly melt
In many streams to fatten lower lands,
And light shall spread, and man be liker man
Through all the seasons of the golden year.

. . . .

. . . . . Happy days
Roll onward, leading up the golden year.
Fly, happy, happy sails, and bear the Press :
Fly happy with the mission of the Cross :
Knit land to land, and blowing heavenward
With silks and fruits, and spices, clear of toll,
Enrich the markets of the golden year.

. . . .

Ah ! when shall all men's good
Be each man's rule, and universal Peace
Lie like a shaft of light across the land,
And like a lane of beams athwart the sea,
Through all the circle of the golden year ?

. . . .

Live on, God loves us, . . . well I know
That unto him who works, and feels he works,
This same grand year is ever at the doors.

———

Forward, forward let us range.
Let the great world spin forever down the
ringing grooves of change.

SPRING.

LIKE souls that balance joy and pain
With tears and smiles from heaven again,
The maiden Spring upon the plain
Came in a sunlit fall of rain.

In crystal vapor everywhere
　Blue isles of heaven laughed between,
　And, far in forest-deeps unseen,
　The topmost linden gathered green
From draughts of balmy air.

Sometimes the linnet piped his song;
Sometimes the throstle whistled strong;
Sometimes the sparhawk wheeled along,
　Hushed all the groves from fear of wrong.

By grassy capes with fuller sound
　In curves the yellowing river ran,
　And drooping chestnut-buds began
　To spread into the perfect fan,
Above the teeming ground.

SUMMER.

" SUMMER is coming, summer is coming,
    I know it, I know it, I know it;
Light again, leaf again, life again, love again!"
    Yes, my wild little poet.

Sing the New Year in under the blue,
    Last year you sang it as gladly :
New, new, new, new!   Is it then *so* new
    That you should carol so madly ?

Love   again,   song   again,   nest   again,   young
        again !
    Never a prophet so crazy !
And hardly a daisy as yet, little friend,
    See, there is hardly a daisy.

"Here again, here, here, here, happy year ! "
    O, warble unchidden, unbidden !
Summer is coming, is coming, my dear,
    And all the winters are hidden.

THE DEATH OF THE OLD YEAR.

I.

FULL knee-deep lies the winter snow
  And the winter winds are wearily sighing;
Toll ye the church-bell sad and slow,
And tread softly and speak low,
  For the old year lies a-dying.
    Old Year, you must not die,
    You came to us so readily,
    You lived with us so steadily,
    Old Year, you shall not die.

II.

He lieth still: he doth not move;
  He will not see the dawn of day,
He hath no other life above.
He gave me a friend, and a true, true-love,
  And the New Year will take 'em away.
    Old Year, you must not go;
    So long as you have been with us,
    Such joy as you have seen with us,
    Old Year, you shall not go.

III.

He frothed his bumpers to the brim;
  A jollier year we shall not see.

But, though his eyes are waxing dim,
And though his foes speak ill of him,
  He was a friend to me.
    Old Year, you shall not die,
    We did so laugh and cry with you,
    I've half a mind to die with you,
    Old Year, if you must die.

IV.

He was full of joke and jest —
  But all his merry quips are o'er ;
To see him die, across the waste
His son and heir doth ride post-haste,
  But he'll be dead before.
    Every one for his own ;
    The night is starry and cold, my friend,
    And the New Year, blithe and bold, my friend,
    Comes up to take his own.

v.

How hard he breathes ! over the snow
  I heard just now the crowing cock ;
The shadows flicker to and fro ;
The cricket chirps ; the light burns low ;
  'Tis nearly twelve o'clock.
    Shake hands before you die,

Old Year, we'll dearly rue for you;
What is it we can do for you?
Speak out before you die.

VI.

His face is growing sharp and thin;
　Alack! our friend is gone.
Close his eyes: tie up his chin,
Step from the corpse, and let him in
　That standeth there alone,
　And waiteth at the door.
There's a new foot on the floor, my friend,
And a new face at the door, my friend,
A new face at the door.

———

I DOUBT not through the ages,
　One increasing purpose runs,
And the thoughts of men are widened
　With the process of the suns.

———

OLD AND NEW.

RING out, wild bells, to the wild sky,
　The flying cloud, the frosty light:
　The year is dying in the night;
Ring out, wild bells, and let him die.

Ring out the old, ring in the new,
　Ring, happy bells, across the snow;
　The year is going, let him go;
Ring out the false, ring in the true.

Ring out the grief that saps the mind,
　For those that here we see no more;
　Ring out the feud of rich and poor,
Ring in redress to all mankind.

Ring out a slowly dying cause,
　And ancient forms of party strife;
　Ring in the nobler modes of life,
With sweeter manners, purer laws.

Ring out the want, the care, the sin,
　The faithless coldness of the times;
　Ring out, ring out my mournful rhymes,
But ring the fuller minstrel in.

Ring out false pride in place and blood,
　The civic slander and the spite;
　Ring in the love of truth and right,
Ring in the common love of good.

Ring out old shapes of foul disease;
　Ring out the narrowing lust of gold;
　Ring out the thousand wars of old,
Ring in the thousand years of peace.

Ring in the valiant man and free,
　The larger heart, the kindlier hand;
　Ring out the darkness of the land,
Ring in the Christ that is to be.

Part Fourth.

NUGGETS OF GOLD.

No help but prayer,
A breath that fleets beyond the world
And touches Him that made it.

———

GOD's finger touched him, and he slept.

———

THE man is proven by the hour.

———

THOROUGHLY to believe in one's own self,
So one's self be thorough, were to do great
    things.

———

WHEN men are tost
On tides of strong opinion, and not sure
Of their own selves, they are wroth with their
    own selves
And thence with others.

———

AT times the small black fly upon the pane
May seem the black ox of the distant plain.

A SMILE abroad is oft a scowl at home.

—

THE miserable have no medicine
But only Hope.

—

SWEET is it to have done the thing one ought,
When fallen on darker ways.

—

LIGHT coin, the tinsel clink of compliment.

—

I STARTED once, . . .
Resolved on noble things, and strove to speak
As when a great thought strikes along the
　　　brain,
And flushes all the cheek.

—

THE smell of violets, hidden in the green.

—

THE star-like sorrows of immortal eyes.

—

　　SHE did not weep,
But o'er her meek eyes came a happy mist
Like that which kept the heart of Eden green
Before the useful trouble of the rain.

AND indeed — This work wrought upon himself
After a life of violence, seems to me
A thousand-fold more great and wonderful
Than if a knight of mine, risking his life,
Should make an onslaught single on a realm
Of robbers, though he slew them one by one
And were himself nigh wounded to the death.

WHO are wise in love
Love most, say least. . . .
Silence is wisdom . . .

HE, from his exceeding manfulness
And pure nobility of temperament,
Wroth to be wroth at such a worm, refrained
From ev'n a word.

WORDS are not always what they seem.

GRATEFUL is the noise of noble deeds
To noble hearts.

" A MAIDEN is a tender thing,
And best by her that bore her understood."

His very face with change of heart is changed.

———

Most blameless is he, centered in the sphere
Of common duties, decent not to fail
In offices of tenderness.

———

A square-set man and honest; and his eyes
An out-door sign of all the warmth within
Smiled with his lips — a smile beneath a cloud;
But Heaven had meant it for a sunny one.

———

A babe — pretty bud! Lily of the vale! half-
opened bell of the woods!

———

Trust that those we call the dead
Are breathers of an ampler day
For ever nobler ends.

———

Though my lips may breathe adieu
I cannot think the thing farewell.

———

The new day comes, the light
Dearer for night, as dearer thou for faults
Lived over.

MORN, in the white wake of the morning-star,
Came furrowing all the orient into gold.

———

GOLD spoils all — Love is the only gold.

———

THE lightnings that we think are only Heaven's
Flash sometimes out of earth against the
    heavens

·   ·   ·   ·   ·   ·   ·   ·   ·

We are self-uncertain creatures, and we may,
Yea, even when we know not, mix our spites
And private hates with our defense of Heaven.

———

EARN well the thrifty months, nor wed
Raw Haste, half-sister to Delay.

———

WISDOM is to know the worst at first.

———

    FRESH and sweet
As the first flower no bee has ever tried.

———

THIS truth within thy mind rehearse,
That in a boundless universe
Is boundless better, boundless worse.

OLD men must die, or the world would grow
mouldy.

———

GREAT deeds cannot die,
They with the sun and moon renew their light,
Forever blessing those that look on them.

———

THERE is nothing upon earth more miserable
than she that has a son and sees him err.

———

WELCOME turns a cottage to a palace.

———

BETTER a man without riches, than riches without a man.

———

LISTEN — overhead
Fluting and piping and luting
" Love, love, love " —
Those sweet tree-cupids half-way up in heaven —
The birds . . .
" Love, love, love, love," what merry madness —
listen.

———

GIVE to the poor,
Ye give to God, He is with us in the poor.

AMBITION is like the sea-wave, which the more
    you drink
The more you thirst.

Is strength the less strength when hand in hand
    with grace?

ACTION and re-action —
The miserable see-saw of our child-world.

To do him any wrong was to beget
A kindness from him, for his heart was rich,
Of such fine mould, that if you sow'd therein
The seed of Hate, it blossom'd Charity.

Do you good to all
As much as in you lieth. Hurt no man more
Than you would harm your living natural brother
Of the same roof, same heart. If any do,
Albeit he thinks himself at home with God,
Of this be sure, he is whole worlds away.

THE parting of a husband and a wife
Is like the cleaving of a heart.

IT is the heat and narrowness of the cage
That makes the captive testy ; with free wing
The world were all an Araby.

————

IF a man
Wastes himself among women, how should he
    love
A woman, as a woman should be loved ?

————

WILD natures need wise curbs.

————

THE chance of noble deeds will come and go
Unchallenged, while you follow wandering fires
Lost in the quagmire.

————

THE jewel of a loyal heart.

————

AND one . . . loved him much beyond the
    rest,
And honor'd him, and wrought into his heart,
A way by love that waken'd love within
To answer that which came.

————

ONE will crown thee king
Far in the spiritual city.

EVERY man, for the sake of the great blessed
Mother in Heaven, and for the love of his own
little mother on earth, should handle all womankind gently, and hold them in all honor. . . .

OBEDIENCE is the bond of rule.

A MOTHER'S eye,
That beam of dawn upon the opening flower.

TIME! if his backward-working alchemy
Should change this gold to silver, why, the silver
Were dear as gold, the wrinkle as the dimple.

How should you love if you mistrust your love?

How often justice drowns
Between the law and letter of the law!

ENID easily believed
Like simple, noble natures, credulous
Of what they long for, good in friend or foe,
There most in those who most have done them
    ill.

SELF-REVERENCE, self-knowledge, self-control,
These three alone lead life to sovereign power.

———

BECAUSE right is right, to follow right
Were wisdom in the scorn of consequence.

———

I HAVE not made the world, and He that made
    it will guide.

———

A LITTLE thing may harm a wounded man.

———

A DOUBTFUL throne is ice on summer seas.

———

           As the tree
Stands in the sun and shadows all beneath,
So in the light of great eternity
Life eminent creates the shade of death.

———

         THAT gentleness,
Which, when it weds with manhood, makes a
    man.

———

SWEETLY gleamed her eyes behind her tears
Like sunlight on the plain behind a shower.

HOWE'ER it be, it seems to me,
    'Tis only noble to be good;
Kind hearts are more than coronets,
    And simple faith than Norman blood.

———

I LEFT him with peace on his face — that
sweet, other-world smile, which will be reflected
in the spiritual body among the angels.

———

    THE years with change advance;
If I make dark my countenance
I shut my life from happier chance.

———

ARE there thunders moaning in the distance?
Are there specters moving in the darkness?
Trust the Hand of Light will lead her people,
Till the thunders pass, the specters vanish,
And the Light is Victor, and the darkness
Dawns into the Jubilee of the Ages.